Damascus Road Experience

A Quest for Great Faith and Godliness

Jeffrey Sakas

© 2022 Maudlin Pond Press, LLC

All rights reserved. No part of this publication may be reproduced, stored in a retrieval system or transmitted in any form or by any means, electronic, mechanical, photo copying, recording or otherwise without the prior permission of the publisher and author or in accordance with the provisions of the copyright, designs and patents act 1988 or under the terms of any license permitting limited copying issued by the copyright licensing agency.

Published by:

Maudlin Pond Press, LLC
PO Box 53, Tybee Island, Georgia 31328, USA

ISBN: 979-8-9857239-4-6
eBook ISBN: 979-8-9857239-5-3

All references to the Bible are to the New International Version©. Zondervan NIV© study Bible (K L Baker edition; full rev. edition.) (2011). Zondervan

Scripture taken from the Holy Bible, New International Version© NIV©. Copyright 1973, 1978, 1984, 2011 by Biblica, Inc™. Used by permission of Zondervan. All rights reserved worldwide. www.zondervan.com the NIV and New International Version are trademarks registered in the United States Patent and Trademark office by Biblica, Inc.™

This book is dedicated to my beloved
Patavia Danielle Bean

Preface

I often tell people that I was in the Navy until I was 13 years old. In truth my family lived on or near Navy bases because my father was in the Navy until I was 13. My father had a natural curiosity concerning scientific matters and would often treat me and my sister with the purchase of microscopes and telescopes for us to look at both the stars and single celled animals. I think that experience instilled a natural curiosity concerning scientific phenomenon in my life. I often try to read scientific magazines, books concerning the latest discussion of physics, biological discoveries, nature and astronomy. The other night I was watching the Ken Burns documentary concerning Benjamin Franklin. That documentary led me to wonder if there is a connection between the physical realm and our spiritual selves. I think it does.

When I wrote this book The United States and all the world was involved in the COVID-19 pandemic. That pandemic has had a profound influence on the lives of millions of people throughout the world. We have gone through waves of variants that seems to never end. Science has crafted vaccines in order to combat that sickness. From a spiritual standpoint the world is watching with horror the atrocities that are being inflicted on the Ukrainian population by Russian invaders and terrorists. The evil that is in the hearts of men seem to have no bounds when you consider that war. It is my belief that not only is there a physical warfare that is raging in this world but that there is also a spiritual warfare that is going on all around us, and we can see physical manifestations of evil in the way people are mistreated.

I wrote this book in order to explain what I believe is a Christian's perspective concerning some of these issues. I have emphasized the teachings of Jesus Christ especially his Sermon on the Mount (Matthew 5-7) and how that teaching of Jesus applies to those of us who strive for greater faith and godliness.

It is my hope that the words of Jesus and the influence of Jesus on the life of the apostle Paul will be of help to those that take up the cross to follow our Lord and savior.

Table of Contents

1. Inertia 1
2. Acts of the Commended 14
   - i. Abel's Pure Heart 18
   - ii. Enoch's Diligence 21
   - iii. Noah's Perseverance 23
   - iv. Abraham's Meekness 25
   - v. Jacob the Peacemaker 28
   - vi. Joseph's Mercy 30
   - vii. Moses Endured (Insults and all kinds of evil) 32
   - viii. The Beatitudes 37
3. Living the Adventure 38
   - i. Availability 38
   - ii. Consciousness 39
   - iii. Expectation 43
   - iv. Seeking 45
   - v. Preparation 47
   - vi. Curiosity 51
   - vii. Fake religion 52
   - viii. Being fooled and temptation to believe .. 53
   - ix. Discernment 55
   - x. Humility 56
   - xi. Anxiety 57
   - xii. The Golden Rule 57
   - xiii. Access to the Holy Spirit 58
   - xiv. Spiritual Gifts 61
   - xv. Service 63
   - xvi. Trusting 67
4. The Nature of Evil 72
   - i. Physical, Mental and Spiritual Evil 72

	ii.	Physical Evil 72
	iii.	Mental Evil 73
	iv.	Spiritual Evil 74
	v.	Is Evil a Part of God's Creation?............ 75
	vi.	Jesus's Life and the Presence of Evil 81
	vii.	Existentialism.. 87

5. Living A Perfect Life 94

6. The Necessity of Christian Fellowship..... 98

7. Forgive Me As I Forgive Those Who Trespass Against Me............................ 107

8. People That Have Pure Hearts 112

9. The Role of a Peacemaker 117

10. Don't Worry Be Happy 121

11. Asking, Seeking, Knocking 128

12. Predestination or Free Will 134

13. Personal Evangelism 139

14. Not All Who Call Me Lord Will Be Saved 148

15. Do We All Have a Spiritual Life? 153

16. I Have Joy Down in My Heart 159

17. The Wisdom That Comes From God 164

18. Following Jesus 171

19. Acknowledgement 179

Chapter 1
Inertia

In the 9th Chapter of the book of Acts of the Apostles, Dr. Luke provides the story of the conversion of Saul. Saul, a devout Jew, studied law with one of the most highly respected legal scholars of his day. As a Jew, Saul believed at that time in history, that the Jews were the chosen people and that any deviation from Judaism as a religion, by Jews, fell into the category of blasphemy and therefore was punishable by death. As an aside, Jews, at that moment in history, believed that they were religiously and morally superior to all other people; and gave the derogatory label of "Gentile" to all non-Jews. Saul undoubtedly believed that he was morally and spiritually superior to those who were followers of Jesus whether they were Jews or Gentiles. After all the main charge leveled against Jesus by the Jewish authorities at his trial just before his crucifixion, was that He had committed blasphemy by claiming to be the Son of God. Additionally, as a Jew, Saul naturally felt himself superior to all Gentiles (non-Jews). As a good Jew, Saul would have daily thanked God that he was not a slave, a woman, or a Gentile.

Saul is first mentioned in the New Testament when he was present at the stoning of Stephen by Jewish leaders within a relatively short time after Jesus's crucifixion. In that vignette Saul, as a lawyer and a member of the Pharisee party, is seen holding the coats of other Pharisees who were stoning Stephen to death. Stephen had been selected as a deacon, to minister among the followers of Jesus, and was tasked with distributing food and sustenance to the widows and poor. Stephen was selected to be a deacon by the original disciples that Jesus called to that position during Jesus earthly ministry. It was said of Stephen that he was an exceptional person; fully devoted to Jesus. As Stephen was dying, he asked God to forgive those who were putting him to death.

As a result of his membership in the Pharisee party Saul, or as he was later known Paul, received letters from the chief priests of the Jews to persecute the followers of Jesus. Luke states that Saul's hatred of those of "The Way" (the name for early Christians) was white-hot. One of Saul's assignments was to travel to Damascus in order to persecute the Jewish followers of Jesus that had fled from Jerusalem to escape the persecution of the Pharisees. Armed with this warrant from the Jewish Sanhedrin (those in charge of enforcing Jewish law), Saul was traveling to Damascus in order to arrest the followers of Jesus and return them to Jerusalem when he was stopped by a brilliant white light and the words of an unknown speaker.

Saul met Jesus. The dazzling white light blinded Saul and those that were with him also were overcome by the brightness. Only Saul however heard the words of Jesus. The Bible records that Jesus said to Saul, "Saul, Saul why do you persecute me? It is hard for you to kick against the goads." (Acts 9:4) Saul replied, "Who are you?" The reply came "I am Jesus whom you have come to persecute." As a result of this encounter Saul was trembling and astonished and blind. Jesus told Saul to go into Damascus and he would receive further instructions. The men that were with Saul, knew that something had happened to Saul but saw no one. They led Saul by hand to the house of Judas on Straight Street in Damascus because Saul was blinded by his encounter with Jesus. There Saul in his blindness and state of confusion, prayed.

While praying Saul received a vision that he would be visited by a man by the name of Ananias. Perhaps simultaneously, Ananias received a vision from God that he was to go down to Straight Street, find a blind man by the name of Saul of Tarsus, and take him under his wing. We can only surmise that God had decided that He needed the talents of Saul for the spread of the gospel. By the time of Ananias' visit, Saul had been sitting at Judas' house for three days. The story indicates that he had neither eaten nor bathed and that he was still blind. When Ananias showed up, he touched Saul's eyes and something like scales immediately came off his eyes and he was able to see. Saul did exactly what any of us would do, he had something to eat got himself ready to travel and accompanied Ananias to Ananias' house. What Paul was about to find out was that he had been selected to be an Apostle of Jesus and that Jesus had selected him for a special mission. Paul also found out that Jesus did not fool around.

Much of the remainder of the book of Acts tells the story of Paul's ministry and missionary journeys from Antioch to Rome itself. Shortly after Paul's encounter with Jesus on the road to Damascus, not only did Saul become known as Paul but his life changed directions. Paul's life change was dramatic. You could say with a great deal of accuracy that Paul went from being the chief persecutor of Jesus to one of the most influential supporters of Jesus. As the story unfolds Paul goes from chief persecutors of those who follow Jesus to spreading the gospel especially to Gentiles. Along the way Paul was beaten, jailed, run out of towns, and martyred because of his faith in Jesus Christ. This drastic change occurred because of Paul's Damascus Road encounter with Jesus Christ.

You may ask yourself, is it necessary to have a Damascus Road like experience in my life in order to come to a realization of Jesus call to "deny yourself and take up your cross and follow me?" Matthew 16:23-25, Luke 9:23-25 and Mark 8:34.

Recently, I became fascinated with the idea of inertia. In Newton's "First Law of Motion," he describes the inherent property of objects in motion to stay in motion and those objects at rest to stay at rest. In order for any object to change the state of its motion or non-motion an outside force must be applied to that object to change either its velocity, or lack thereof, and its direction. The question then becomes, does this "First Law of Motion" (that we now refer to as inertia) apply to physical, emotional, and spiritual aspects of our lives. You could say to yourself "It certainly appeared that Paul was going in one direction and when he met Jesus the direction and velocity of his life changed so that Saul became Paul, and that force changed the course of Western Civilization."

The outside force that changes our lives and causes us to go in either one direction or another could be referred to as a Damascus Road experience. Sometimes, the Damascus Road experience is overwhelming, and it is impossible to miss, as in Paul's experience. Sometimes however, the Damascus Road experience may be more subtle, and we do not become aware that an outside force is changing our direction and velocity. After all, one of the most natural forces of nature that causes objects in motion to change their inertia is friction. Friction in the physical realm is the resistance that one surface or object encounters when moving over another object. From an emotional standpoint friction is a conflict or animosity; friction may cause a clash of wills, a change in temperament, or opinion. Sometimes it is almost impossible to discern when an outside force is causing a change in our lives.

How do you overcome spiritual inertia?

In Paul's case the direction and velocity of his life was met by a blinding light and the voice of Jesus telling him to "quit kicking against the goads," that is; stop going in the wrong direction, do not resist God's call on your life, move in a direction that is set out for you by Jesus. More often however, it is the still small voice of God revealing, to those who are attuned to his leading, that a change of direction is necessary. Perhaps this hypothesis can be stated as follows: a change in direction is necessary in order to become aware of the direction to which God has chosen for your life; a direction that brings us into conformity with the call of Jesus to deny ourselves and take up our cross in order to follow Him.

You might also ask yourself, "Is there just one Damascus Road experience in each person's life or is there many such experiences?" Can we go in the right direction, lose our momentum and be diverted from the course that has been set for us, who believe in the authority and grace of Jesus Christ? After all Paul was white-hot in his persecution of Jesus followers. He changed his course by 180° and became a missionary and writer of Christian philosophy that became the most influential statement of the power of Jesus Christ on the lives of men and women since Jesus was sent to mankind. Paul's influence on Christianity seems to have taken place as a result of one significant encounter with Jesus. I suspect, however, that it is more likely that inertia is overcome by a process that causes slight changes of direction and velocity over longer periods of our lives. At least that has been my experience.

That is not to say that the inertia of our lives can or cannot reach a critical mass at any particular time. Sometimes, inertia can cause stagnation or an inability to move. On the other hand, the motion and velocity in our lives that is moving us in the wrong direction must be overcome for our own survival.

Take for example the curious case of a man by the name of Jonah. Jonah had a clear call from God, a Damascus Road experience. Jonah was told to go up to Nineveh and preach repentance to the Ninevites. Jonah recognized that the call was from God. Jonah evidently clearly heard God's call to go preach but because he had preconceived ideas that any effort that he made at changing the minds of the warlike people of Nineveh was futile, Jonah wanted to stay home and watch football. When God insisted that Jonah get up and go to Nineveh the Bible says that Jonah went down to Joppa and got down in the bottom of a boat that was heading in the opposite direction of Nineveh.

When a storm came up and threatened to sink the boat, Jonah admitted to the group of sailors who were trying to keep the boat afloat, that the storm was directed at him because he had run from God's instructions. Jonah jumped overboard and went down into the sea. Eventually Jonah went down into the belly of the great fish. After three days of being fish bait the fish had enough of Jonah and spit him out on the shore.

If the story Jonah and the fish had ended right there things would have been exceptional; but that's not the end of the story. Jonah eventually made it to Nineveh and preached repentance. To his astonishment the King and all the people repented, and Israel was spared from the invasion of the Ninevites. Now you think the story has come to a conclusion, but it has not. Jonah went outside the city sat under a tree and was unhappy that Nineveh had repented. The Bible does not record what happened to Jonah after his successful Nineveh Crusade. We can only guess that Jonah was not asked to preach anymore because that is the last time we hear about Jonah. But we can rest assured that the attitude exemplified by the reluctant preacher is an example of a negative response to a clear call to serve by our Lord.

Many times, we are not aware of the life forces that either must be overcome to get us going in the right direction, or that allows us to exert the effort necessary for us to escape from being a couch potato. For example, in her book *Leadership in Turbulent Times*, Doris Kearns Goodwin describes in each of the historical characters that she writes about; Abraham Lincoln, Theodore Roosevelt, Franklin Delano Roosevelt, and Lyndon Johnson, particular critical events that caused profound changes in the lives of these notable men, each of whom later became the President of the United States.

For Abraham Lincoln (who Carl Sandberg described the saddest man in three counties, and who was so funny that he could make a cat laugh) who was prone to suffer from melancholy from his childhood, it was his defeat in his second run for Congress that caused an overall feeling of rejection that prompted Lincoln to turn inward. Lincoln's friends put him on a suicide watch and took all the knives and sharp edges out of his apartment. It was when Lincoln overcame his depression (his Damascus Road experience), that acted as the catalyst that allowed him to use his innate strategic political abilities, obtain the nomination of the Republican Party for President in 1860 and then lead the country through the nightmare of the Civil War. Lincoln's Emancipation Proclamation and the passage of the 13th amendment to the United States Constitution just before Lincoln's assignation was a start down the road to freedom for millions of former slaves.

Theodore Roosevelt, who suffered chronic health issues during his childhood, had his Damascus Road experience when his mother and wife died within a day of each other. Teddy Roosevelt overcame that crisis by retreating to work as a cowboy in Montana. He used that experience to rehabilitate his health and set his mind on his political career. Theodore Roosevelt emerged to become Governor of New York, Vice President and then President of the United States after the assassination of President McKinley. With Teddy Roosevelt's leadership the United States was able to overcome potential economic disaster by breaking up monopolies and insisting that large corporations act in a more humane manner.

Franklin Roosevelt, a distant cousin of Theodore Roosevelt, contracted polio while he was still a young man. Even though FDR had served as Undersecretary of the Navy prior to his illness, he believed that he was destined for greater service to America. FDR was paralyzed and lost the use of his legs for the remainder of his life. He could have called it quits, but instead faced with this crisis, went on to overcome his disabilities. At the height of the Great Depression, it was Franklin Roosevelt's leadership that initiated government programs designed to fix a broken banking system, put millions of unemployed Americans into productive jobs and get the economy of the United States moving again. It was FDR's leadership after his crisis (Damascus Road experience) that brought the United States through most of World War II. It was also as a result of FDR's leadership that the security net of Social Security gives older Americans at least a modest pension.

Lyndon Johnson's family lost their home and land during the Great Depression of the 1930s. Johnson attended a small college in Texas and became a teacher in a public school in which many of the students were from the Hispanic minority. LBJ worked tirelessly to advance his students participation in the educational process. Eventually, LBJ ran for Congress and was elected. Johnson was instrumental in bringing electrification to his rural district by eliciting favors from more prestigious members of the House of Representatives. Johnson's goal in life was to become president of the United States. In the early-1940s Johnson seized an opportunity to run for the United States Senate but was defeated. That political setback caused Johnson's Damascus Road experience. Johnson returned to Congress and seemed to turn inward. It appeared that Johnson only wanted to exploit his position for personal gain. It was only when Johnson was able to overcome his emotional depression, caused by his defeat for the Senate seat (Johnson's Damascus Road experience) that he was able to learn valuable life lessons from his election defeat. He became a senator and then used his superior political ability to provide a means to get the 1957 Voting Rights Act passed. That act started a legislative initiative to overcome the system in the United States that failed to include African Americans in the political process. The passage of the 1957 Voting Rights Act required a skill that only Lyndon Johnson seemed to possess. The Voting Rights Act set the stage for the 1964 Civil Rights Act that was the significant political focal point of the Johnson presidency. Overcoming a political setback was necessary in Johnson's life to advance the quest for equality in America.

Doris Kearns Goodwin provides a historical basis in the lives of these four former American presidents to confirm that each had to overcome a crisis in their lives to reach their full potential. There are probably many more examples that we can explore in order to answer the questions raised above. That is; is it necessary to have a Damascus Road experience in order to overcome the inertia in our own lives? Additionally, can we recognize that we have had a Damascus Road experience in order to confirm that we are heading in the right direction in our life, and can therefore, claim the grace that Jesus intends for each of us to obtain?

Also, we should examine if there is the necessity of having a Damascus Road experience to have a meaningful and consistent relationship with Jesus. Prior to Jesus bursting onto the scene, John the Baptist preached repentance and baptism as an expression of a changed life. Matthew 3:1-3. Similarly, after Jesus fasted in the wilderness for 40 days and was tempted, Jesus' ministry was initiated by a call to repentance because the Kingdom of God was and is nearby. Matthew 4:1-17. When we become Christians, especially in the Baptist tradition of faith (the denomination to which the writer belongs), we are called upon to recognize our sinful nature and repent. (Baptist generally refers to this process as "believer's baptism" because repentance is a deliberate choice that requires a knowing recognition and a confession of our sinfulness). While our salvation is complete at the time of our repentance, confession, and a request for Jesus to forgive our sins and enter into our lives; that does not guarantee that we are fully developed and useful in the expansion of God's Kingdom.

Salvation is a deliberate and often mysterious response to the call of Jesus and is open to all people. Paul in 1 Timothy 2:4 tells us that we are all called to salvation and to the knowledge of truth. However, it is only in the testing of our faith and the tempering of our belief that we can advance into being productive members of His Family.

Recently, in the Ken Burns documentary *Country Music*, the songwriter/performer Kris Kristofferson discusses his salvation experience. He was brought to a church just outside Nashville, Tennessee by a fellow performer. Kristofferson stated that he did not think that he was aware of everything that was going on around him when the pastor of the church invited people to come forward and receive salvation through Jesus Christ. Kristofferson said that he was barely aware of what prompted him to get up from his seat walk the aisle and accept Jesus into his life. The amount of faith necessary in order to hear the call for salvation is mystical and mysterious. For Kristofferson his leap of faith resulted in his becoming a Christian. Country Music, Episode Six, September 23, 2019.

On the other hand, it is the change that occurs after testing and tempering that brings us to a Damascus Road experience. In Jonah's case the tempering and testing did not seem to take hold. You would think that after Jonah had been in the belly of the fish for three days that his attitude would have had a serious adjustment. That does not seem to be the case, however.

We would also be remiss if we did not consider life-changing experiences from a negative point of view. It is likely that for every positive life-changing experience that occurs when anyone comes to the crossroads of their lives that there are many life-changing events that drive people in a downward spiral. Even Jesus admonishes us that "while many are called few are chosen" Matthew 22:14. Missed opportunities litter the paths that we follow throughout our life. John Bunyan in *Pilgrim's Progress* describes the scenes before and after Christian stands at the cross. In Bunyan's classic book many fail to escape the Giant of Despair. Also, along the way many fall into the slough of despond where a pilgrim's sins cannot be overcome. It was only by the help of the Angel that Christian was able to escape the slough of despond and again set his feet on the right path to the Celestial City. While Pilgrim's Progress is an allegory of the progress individuals make towards heaven in their lives, in fact many lives are lost along the pathway.

When we are faced with difficult decisions, that may or may not have the most profound effects on our lives, we have the choice of responding either positively or negatively. At times we may fall into a period of doubt and despair, the slough of despond. Certainly, in the lives of the four presidents (described above) each went through a period of self-doubt, each turned inward, and each even faced depression before they eventually overcame the crisis in their life. I wonder if Jesus called others to be apostles who turned down that opportunity. I wonder if for every Paul that heard Jesus' call and responded in a positive manner, there were and are others who hear the call and do not respond or reject the call. You may ask yourself what causes some people to respond positively and what causes some people to respond negatively? The answer to that question is difficult at best and may be impossible to answer completely. The answer may depend on the amount of faith that we can muster to advance our own Damascus Road experience.

In Matthew 6:30 Jesus admonishes his disciples concerning the worries of the world by saying to them "oh ye of little faith." What does Jesus mean by telling his disciples that they have little faith? Is there an antidote for those suffering from little faith? In contrast the writer of Hebrews tells us at Hebrews 11:1 that "Now faith is the substance of things hoped for, the evidence of things not seen." The writer of Hebrews goes on to give us the Hall of Fame of those who have demonstrated great faith. In each of the examples given in Hebrews 11, God called, and each named individual responded positively. As each individual responded there was some initial resentence but there is no indication of doubt or skepticism. Neither of the members of the faithful "Who's Who" questioned God's intentions or authority to direct that individual's actions. What drives some to hear and respond positively? What is the defining act that separates those with little faith from the faithful hall of fame? A careful look at the life of each of the members of the "Who's Who" of Hebrews 11 can give us some clues about the difference between great faith and little faith.

Chapter 2
Acts of the Commended

In Hebrews 11 the writer consistently talks about those who received a commendation from God. In fact, in verse 1 the writer tells us that we are to consider the commendation of the ancients. A commendation is recognition of right behavior, exemplary performance, or a willingness to go above and beyond the ordinary.

Hank Berthalo wanted to be a soldier when he got out of high school. He joined the Army during the years that the United States was involved in the war in Vietnam. Hank was sent to Vietnam and did well. The Army recognized his abilities and sent him to West Point. After graduation he was sent back to Vietnam and after a while, he was promoted to the rank of Captain. Hank commanded a company of men who were assigned to fight in that portion of Vietnam referred to as the Iron Triangle. Hank's company was engaged by the Viet Cong and eventually the enemy overran his position. Recognizing the hopelessness of the condition that he and his company were in; Hank called a rocket strike down on his own position. Hank was severely wounded but survived. He later received the Congressional Medal of Honor for valor above and beyond the call of duty.

Each of us recognizes that our lives require a certain amount of faith. We have faith that the sun will come up in the morning and it will set in the evening. We have faith that we can overcome hunger by eating and that we can quench our thirst by drinking. We have faith that we can look good by wearing clothes that are tailored to our needs. We have faith that there will be air to breathe and that if we obey the traffic laws, we will not get traffic tickets. In other words, there is a whole lot of matters that we take for granted because we have faith that our previous actions meet the needs that we have. We all have faith in many things. I would characterize the faith that each of us has that allows us to get up in the morning and go about our daily activities as being an intuitive faith.

The faith that allows us to buy a house or car on credit because we believe that we will receive a continuing paycheck is a higher level of faith, but that faith is not something for which we could be commended.

Certainly, when we accept Jesus Christ as our Savior because we have faith that He alone can save us from our sins, we have stepped out from the mundane into a realm of spiritual faithfulness that requires a belief system in which we understand that the universe was formed by God's command. That amount of faith requires a belief that God in fact is in control of the universe. Therefore, the belief that God is in control of the universe is fundamental to the amount of faith necessary to become a Christian. Spiritual faithfulness starts with a certainty that there is a God, that God knows me, and that I can discern what God requires of me. As I said before, the cause of the amount of faithfulness necessary to believe in God is a mystery.

E.O. Wilson the Pulitzer prize-winning myrmecologist in his book *The Meaning of Human Existence* suggests that religion (generally the belief in God) has been hardwired into our brains by evolutionary forces, but a belief in God can be overcome by scientific observation. Wilson believes that there is no necessity for a belief in God because science is sufficient to solve the mysteries of life. Wilson equates religion to a belief in magic. When humankind cannot explain certain mysteries, they attribute the explanation to either magic or religion. Eventually, Professor Wilson argues, humans will evolve to a point that there is no longer a need for a belief in God. Additionally, we all know people who choose not to believe that there is a God. Some non-believers are very vocal in their denial of the existence of God, some even appear to relish their denial.

Jesus stated at John 14: 6-11 "I am the way and the truth and the life. No one comes to the Father except through me. If you really know me, you will know my Father as well. From now on, you do know Him and have seen Him." Philip said, "Lord, show us the Father and that will be enough for us." Jesus replied: "Don't you know me, Philip even after I have been among you for such a long time? Anyone who has seen me has seen the Father. How can you say, "show us the Father?" Don't you believe that I am in the Father, and that the Father is in me? The words that I say to you I do not speak on my own authority. Rather, it is the Father, living in me, who is doing His work. Believe me when I say that I am in the Father, and the Father is in me; or at least believe on the evidence of the works themselves..."

Much later John, the disciple of Jesus, in his letters explains that he had personally been with Jesus and that he can attest that Jesus is truly the son of God. 1 John 5:14. Additionally, the Bible explains that there were many witnesses of the life of Jesus and His ultimate resurrection from the dead. Paul in his epistles also states that he had direct evidence of the nature of God through the revelation of Jesus. It is therefore axiomatic that for Christians a belief in God is also a belief that Jesus' claim of divinity is a certainty.

Archaeologist have searched for empirical evidence to either prove or disprove the existence of Jesus. Kristin Romy an archaeologist in her own right, in the November 28, 2017, edition of *National Geographic*, traces the archaeological evidence concerning Jesus. In her interviews with other archaeologist, she came to the conclusion that no serious archaeologist would dispute the fact of the historical Jesus. The dispute centers on whether historical Jesus was merely an itinerant preacher that became a folk legend or whether the claims of the Gospel that Jesus is the incarnate Son of God are accurate. The archaeological answer to that dispute cannot be accurately answered. The archaeological evidence seems to suggest that while the accounts of Jesus deeds in the New Testament cannot be confirmed neither can they be disregarded. Skeptics discount the treasure trove of archaeological findings that support the existence of a historical Jesus. Christians visit the historical sites surrounding the life of Jesus and pay homage.

It seems that we are left with the conundrum of whether we can be skeptical, doubtful, and without faith; or we can step out in faith and believe that God exists and that we can have a relationship with God. After all, the Bible says that even demons believe in God, and they tremble. James 2:19. What then separates us as believers from non-believers? The answer must be that belief in God requires a measure of faith that is elusive to some and mystical to others. Those that have faith possess their faith through a mystery that cannot be solved by either scientific or empirical evidence. Either you have faith, or you do not. The amount of faith that anyone possesses cannot be quantified except in one's own heart. When we are called to become Christians, we are free to accept Jesus or to reject Jesus. Acceptance while mystical in its very nature requires a leap of faith.

So, we are back to the same question that I raised above; what is the demarcation between persons with little faith and persons with great faith? Additionally, can a person with little faith achieve great faith? Lastly, does achieving great faith require a Damascus Road experience so that we may come to a point in our life that will allow us to overcome the spiritual inertia that can so easily rob us of an experience of greatness?

An examination of those who were commended for their faith is in order.

Abel's Pure Heart

According to Genesis 4 the first children of Adam and Eve were Cain and Abel. (Whether you believe in historical Cain and Able is not necessary in order to derive benefit from this part of the Scripture, as the story and the meaning and lessons that can be derived from the story are evident). After Adam and Eves' children grew into adulthood, the Bible records that God required an offering from each of them and that by faith Abel brought God a more pleasing offering than Cain. Abel was commended as righteous. The story of Cain and Abel does not clearly identify why Abel's offering was more acceptable to God than that of his brother, but we can deduce that Abel's offering was pleasing to God because Abel was a righteous man. Therefore, righteousness is an ingredient of great faith. In order to be counted as having faith that is pleasing to God a Christian must act in a righteous manner.

What is righteousness? The Bible tells us that only God is righteous. See Romans 3:10 and Psalms 145:17. It is axiomatic then that for us to achieve any semblance of righteousness we must take on the attributes of God. Theologically this is referred to as "Godliness." While it is impossible for us to be completely Godlike, Jesus tells us in the Sermon on the Mount (Matthew 5:48) that we are to strive to be perfect even as God is perfect and that those who hunger and thirst after righteousness are blessed (Matthew 5: 6). Therefore, we are to strive to take on the very nature of God. That begs the question of what is the nature of God?

When we were children, we learned that God is good. Later we began to experience God as being a God that cares about us, listens to us, seeks to do good for us, is responsive to our needs, provides for our protection, saves us from our sins, takes on our concerns, teaches us how to communicate with Him, is holy, requires our devotion, is always vigilant, and I am sure that we can think of plenty of other attributes of God that we would like to emulate. What is missing from this listing of the attributes of God is what we would consider to be evil. We can say with certainty that God is good, and He is not evil or capricious. The correct conclusion that we can drive from the fact that there is evil in the world is that there must be a God that is good. We will explore this thought in greater detail later in this book.

In the meantime, we need to get back to the consideration of Abel's righteousness. God accepted Abel's offering because Abel manifested the attributes of Godliness as opposed to Cain's evil intent. How do we know that Cain had an evil intent? Because shortly after Abel made a more acceptable offering, Cain in a fit of rage killed his brother. It seems that there has always been warfare between good and evil and that God accepts the actions of those with the right motive but rejects the actions of those whose motivations are inconsistent with goodness. Abel brought his offering to God with the right motivation. Abel wanted to please God and to live a Godly life. On the other hand, Cain did not please God because his motivation in making an offering to God fell short of God's expectation of a good life. While it is impossible to derive Cain's intentions from the brief narrative that we have in Genesis our experiences with others can give us clues concerning Cain's motivation.

How often have we been confronted with people who never seem to have anything but their own self-interests as the motivation for their actions? Currently, Donald Trump, the former president of the United States, seems to have been so motivated by his own desire for self-aggrandizement that he was willing to sacrifice even the security of the country. I am sure that there are other examples of this type of behavior that each of us has encountered. When I am confronted with those who only have their own personal interest as the motivation for their actions I tend to back away. Even in the closest relationships, including marriage, if one of the parties to the relationship, cares only about their own interest, the relationship is doomed to failure. The exact opposite is the nature of God. "God so loved the world that He gave His only son." And not only did He send Jesus into this world as an example of His love, but Jesus also showed us the love of God by sacrificing Himself for us. My study of the Scriptures shows me that there was no evil, no self-motivation, and no self-aggrandizement in the life of Jesus.

For God to accept Abel's gift and to count him as a righteous person, Abel's motivation in giving his sacrifice was pure. Abel's motivation was to do what was pleasing in God's sight because Abel's heart was in the right place. After all Jesus, in the Sermon on the Mount, said to us "Blessed are the pure in heart for they shall see God" (Matthew 5:8). A pure heart is a heart that has no evil and intends to do what is right and good and to please God.

Enoch's Diligence

In Hebrews 11:5 the writer tells us that by faith Enoch was taken so that he did not experience death. Others attested that before he was taken away that he pleased God. Then unexpectedly, the writer of Hebrews says that if anyone should approach God, that person must believe that God exists and that He rewards those who diligently seek Him. In the book of Genesis, the story of Enoch states that Enoch walked closely with God. Therefore, it is safe to say that Enoch had a close relationship with the Almighty. Enoch's story also includes the notation that Enoch was the father of Methuselah and the great-grandfather of Noah.

To have a close relationship with anyone requires intimacy. In marriage intimacy takes on a wide range of actions. In friendships intimacy requires each party to care about the other person's well-being. The best of friendships can be characterized by a willingness to keep the friendship no matter the circumstances. The word that describes the intimacy required for a great friendship is diligence. Diligence is that sense of determination to keep the friendship going no matter what the cost. In many of the Psalms, the songwriters talk about the consistent, purposeful, tireless love of God. A friend is tireless in his devotion to his friend even when he is bored out of his mind. On the other hand, the writers of many of The Psalms, state that God loves those who are diligent in their pursuit of God. Enoch was singled out by the writer of Hebrews as a person who was diligent in his desire to have a close relationship with God.

In a relationship with God our duty is to be constantly aware that God not only exists but that He is near us and wants to continue the relationship. Therefore, it is the trait of diligence that Enoch displayed in his relationship with God that allowed him to walk closely with God and to be rewarded for his faithfulness.

In Matthew 5: 6 Jesus stated, "Blessed are those who hunger and thirst after righteousness, for they shall be satisfied." Righteousness in this sense is also related to the exact nature of God. Most of us living in the United States do not know what it means to be extremely hungry or thirsty. At the time that Jesus spoke the words in Matthew 5:6 people knew what it meant to be hungry and thirsty. Palestine was a dry and thirsty land. Food was scarce. People spent much of their time pursuing water and sustenance. To pursue righteousness with the same devotion as a hungry and thirsty person meant that the goal of receiving righteousness was the same as sustaining one's own life. Diligence is related very closely to the attitude of a person dying of hunger and thirst in his pursuit of bread and water. The attribute of diligence on the part of Enoch in his relationship with God made Enoch a person who found favor with God and who had the type of faith that is necessary to be considered a person displaying great as opposed to little faith.

Noah's Perseverance

We all pretty much know the story of Noah and the ark. Some of us have even seen the motion picture 2012 in which the world is saved by the building of a series of modern-day arks in the Tibetan mountains by the Chinese in order to save a remnant of humanity. Some of us may even remember the Bill Cosby comedy sketch in which he plays the part of Noah having a conversation with God about building an ark. When God asks Noah how long he can tread water, Noah gets the picture and goes about building even as those who were watching Noah build the ark scoffed at the sight.

Hebrews 11:7 states, "By faith Noah, when warned about things not yet seen, in holy fear built an ark to save his family. By his faith he condemned the world and became heir of the righteousness that is in keeping with faith."

According to the book of Genesis after Enoch, the world went to hell in a handbag. The depravity of humanity became so overwhelming that God had to act. In that depraved society, Noah stood out as a man who respected God and lived a Godly life. For that reason, God warned Noah that a flood was coming and that for him to save his family and all animal life on earth that Noah would have to build an ark that would withstand the coming deluge. God provided the dimensions of the ark and assisted in the gathering of the animals that would be housed in the ark during the flood. Eventually, the flood came. It rained and the earth opened its wells of water to completely flood the world. The Flood then lasted beyond the 40 days and 40 nights and the entire world was flooded. (Interestingly many other stories of creation by Native Americans and other Indigenous people, relate that a flood covered the earth and wiped out much of the population.) Humanity other than those in the ark was destroyed. When the waters began to recede, Noah sent a dove out from the ark in order to determine whether there was dryland. When Noah and his family finally emerged from the ark, Noah prayed and entered into a covenant with God in which God promised not to again destroy the world by flood and made a rainbow as evidence of the covenant between God and the flood survivors. Later, Noah became the first tiller of soil and invented wine.

There are many stories of floods in other cultures. Prior to the compilation of the stories in the Bible, the Mesopotamian epic story of Gilgamesh has a character very similar to Noah who also builds an ark and saved humanity. The Quran also discusses Noah, and the story of the flood can also be found in Hindu scriptures. Many Native American stories discuss the flood and the rejuvenation of life after the flood. There is genomic evidence that the world population at one time shrank to a very few people and then spread in many different directions. The historical context of the account of Noah in the Bible is therefore one of many stories of a great flood that destroyed all but a remnant of the world's population. From this perspective, the story of Noah teaches us lessons concerning how Noah reacted to a warning from God and that he needed to take measures to preserve life.

The writer of Hebrews says that Noah was given a warning of things not yet seen. In other words, Noah relied on a clear message from God and did what God required. How many of us when receiving a message from God, first recognizes that it is a message from God and, secondly act upon that message.

It is not clear how long it took Noah to build the ark but during that time he had to continually believe in the message and act accordingly. The faith of Noah was therefore great because he persevered once he understood God's warning and continued to build an ark based on God's warning.

Hebrews 11:7 continues with these words, "By his faith he (Noah) condemned the world and became heir of the righteousness that is in keeping with faith." While it is unclear what the precise meaning of these words are meant to convey, it seems that Noah by faith turned away from evil so that righteousness could at least have a chance to continue. Therefore, Noah recognized that God had a special plan for which only Noah chose to respond, and Noah would not give into the evil that was in the world. For that reason, Noah is said to be a man of great faith and was commended.

In Matthew 5:3 Jesus says, "Blessed are the poor in spirit, for theirs is the kingdom of heaven." In that regard, a person who is poor in spirit is a person that is totally in need of the intervention of God in their lives. Noah could have chosen to give into the world that was around him in all its depravity. Rather than giving into evil, Noah chose to rely exclusively on God's intervention in his life. Noah persevered in his total reliance on God even though the world around him may have pushed him in a different direction.

Abraham's Meekness

Abraham has a special place in the history of the Jewish people as well as those who practice Islam because Abraham is both the father of Isaac and Ishmael. The Bible indicates that Abram (Abraham's name before he left Mesopotamia to immigrate to a land that he did not know) was called by God and obeyed God's calling. Abraham's story starts in the town of Ur. The biblical account has been somewhat confirmed in archaeological findings that have taken place since World War I. The biblical account tells that God told Abraham to leave and to go to a place that God would show him and that if Abraham obeyed; God would make Abraham the father of many nations. The biblical account indicates that Abraham together with his father Terah and Abraham's wife Sarah (also known as Sarai) left Ur and traveled to Harran where after a substantial period of time, Abraham's father died. By the time of Terah's death Abraham was 75 years old. Archaeological findings indicate that it is probable that Abraham then traveled into what is now modern Turkey, then after another significant amount of time, Abraham and his entourage traveled westward and came into the region we now know as Israel.

In Abraham's caravan was also Abraham's nephew Lot. Eventually, the caravan split, and Lot settled in what became known as Sodom and Gomorrah. Lot was captured by one of the local kings and Abraham and his band of men rescued Lot. After this military operation Abraham was visited by the king of priests, Melchizedek. Thereafter, Abraham was visited by strangers that he took in and fed. It turned out that these men were angelic representatives of God who informed Abraham that despite his age and the age of his wife who is now known as Sarah that he would have legitimate offspring that would become a great nation. Even though Sarah upon hearing that she would bear a child, expressed her doubt of that happening, and laughed out loud. It came to pass that when Abraham was 100 years old and his 90-year-old wife Sarah who had been barren, Sarah gave birth to Isaac the son of Abraham and his wife.

Prior to Isaac's birth, Sarah doubting the promise of God and believing that she would never bear Abraham a child had given her servant, Hagar, to Abraham for the purpose of bearing a child. Hagar gave birth to Ishmael. Ishmael's descendent was Muhammad the great profit of Islam.

After Isaac's birth it seemed that God's promise to Abraham to be the father of a great nation, in this case the Hebrew nation, had come to fruition. The Bible records however that God told Abraham to sacrifice Isaac. In obedience, Abraham took Isaac and prepared to sacrifice his son. The Bible indicates that just as Abraham had raised his arm to strike and kill Isaac God intervened and provided a ram as a substitute sacrifice.

In going through the story of Abraham, the one word that jumps out and characterizes the faithfulness of Abraham is that he was obedient. Obedience is a willingness to follow the direction of the one who is capable of setting out the prescribed action. In this case God spoke to Abraham in a dream and to Abraham's credit Abraham believed that he was being instructed by God and obeyed the instruction.

In the Sermon on the Mount Jesus in Matthew 5:5 states, "Blessed are the meek, for they will inherit the earth." A person is meek when he/she is able and willing to take instruction and comply. In other words, a meek person is an obedient person. The characteristic of Abraham that caused him to be a person of great faith was that he was obedient to God's instruction. Abraham's meekness in that sense was rewarded with the honor of fathering a great nation.

As an aside one cannot diminish the role of Sarah in this discussion. God's messengers told Abraham that, despite his age and the age of his barren wife that she would conceive and give birth to a son. Sarah, the Bible records, went into lol mode. Despite the shock of being told that her 100-year-old husband still had enough left in his tank to want and desire his wife, Sarah doubted that she could become a mother for the first time in her old age. When Sarah conceived and gave birth to Isaac her joy was overwhelming. Sarah's faithfulness, even in the face of doubt, makes her a fitting honoree in the Hebrews 11 Hall of Fame of those with great faith.

Jacob the Peacemaker

Jacob and his brother Esau were twin boys whose father was Isaac, the son of Abraham. The Bible says that Esau was born first, and Jacob was born clutching Esau's heel. Isaac showed favoritism to Esau while Rebecca, Isaac's wife, showed favoritism to Jacob. Of course, this caused problems in the family. Once while Esau had been out hunting Jacob made a pot of lentils stew. Esau was famished and agreed to give up his birthright for a bowl of the porridge. In those days a birthright was an extremely important commodity. The birthright gave preference to the recipient and made him the leader of the family once the chief died.

Esau often provided Isaac with meat while Jacob was more of a mama's boy. When Isaac was old and was about to give his blessing to Esau, Rebecca hatched a scheme in which Jacob pretended to be Esau and tricked Isaac (in fact the name Jacob means deceiver) into giving Jacob the birthright that should have gone to Esau. As a result, there was enmity between Esau and Jacob to the extent that Jacob had to get out of town quickly.

On his way out of town Jacob decided to bed down for the night and in a dream, Jacob was confronted by God (some Bible scholars state that Jacob was actually confronted by Jesus as the Bible states that angels ascended and descended at the place that Jacob spent the night, and that Jacob was confronted by Jesus. In the Gospel of John chapter 1 Jesus tells Nathaniel that he would see Angels ascending and descending referencing that Jesus in fact was the person involved with Jacob in the Genesis story). Jacob thusly had a Damascus Road experience. In that dream Jacob and the divine spirit got into a wrestling match and Jacob would not let go until he received a blessing from God.

Jacob wound up going to Paddan-Aram where he met a woman by the name of Rachel and fell in love. Rachel's father, Laban, promised Jacob that he could marry Rachel if he worked for Laban for seven years. When the seven years were over and the wedding ceremony began Laban substituted his older daughter, Leah for Jacob's intended. The story indicates that Jacob had to work another seven years in order to obtain the right to marry Rachel. By then Jacob had children with Leah but also took Rachel as his second wife. Jacob and Rachel had two sons, Joseph and Benjamin.

When things started getting crowded in Laban's tent, Jacob decided to return to Canaan with his wives, children, herds of sheep, camels and all the rest of his household goods. On the way back to Canaan Jacob had another dream in which God told Jacob that he would no longer be Jacob, but his name would be changed to Israel.

As Jacob's (now Israel's) caravan approached the old stomping grounds, Esau and his men set out to meet his brother. Jacob sent a peace offering to Esau, met Esau and the two of them worked things out. Jesus says that "Blessed are the peacemakers, for they will be called children of God." Matthew 5:9. The descendants of Jacob became the 12 tribes of Israel. One of the attributes of a person with great faith is that they seek peace and are willing to do what is necessary to ensure that peace reigns.

In the Sermon on the Mount Jesus says at Matthew 5:9, "Blessed are the peacemakers for they will be called children of God." A child of God who knows that God loves him/her can exhibit great faith. Obviously, Jacob exhibited great faith by acting on God's instruction and made peace with his brother.

Joseph's Mercy

In the 1950s there was a weekly adventure serial that caused me to go to the movie theater on a weekly basis to find out what was going to happen to Flash Gordon. Flash traveled in outer space and became the captive of the evil ruler of another world whose name was Ming the Merciless. Ming was so evil that he would even dare to sacrifice his own daughter in order to fight against Flash Gordon who was trying to protect the earth. In contrast to Ming the Merciless is Joseph the oldest son of the relationship between Israel, ne Jacob and Rachel.
Joseph had a series of dreams in which he saw that sometime in the future his brothers would become

subservient to him. When Joseph told his brothers about his dream, you might guess their reaction. They were nonplussed.

Additionally, Jacob favored Joseph above his brothers and bought him a coat of many colors. As a result, Joseph's brothers despised Joseph. One time when Joseph was visiting his brothers as they were tending their flocks, Joseph's brothers decided to kill him, but at the last moment, decided to sell him into slavery instead. Joseph wound up being the slave of Potiphar, a government official in Egypt, and eventually wound up in jail because Potiphar's wife wrongly and maliciously accused Joseph of trying to seduce her.

While Joseph was in jail, Pharaoh, the ruler of Egypt, had a dream in which he saw 7 skinny cows eating up seven fat cows. None of the wise men of Egypt could interpret Pharaoh's dream. Because Joseph had a gift from God of dream interpretation, Joseph was summoned to the Pharaoh's house in order to interpret the Pharaoh's dream. Joseph's interpretation was that there would be seven years of great harvests in Egypt followed by seven years of famine.

Everybody in the Pharaoh's house was scratching their heads concerning what to do about the dream except Joseph who knew exactly what to do. During the years of plenty Egypt would store up its grain so that when the famine inevitably struck there would be enough. Not only would the Egyptians benefit but they would be able to sell the excess produce to their surrounding neighbors and become a very wealthy kingdom. The interpretation that Joseph made of Pharaoh's dream came true and Pharaoh made Joseph second in command throughout the entire kingdom.

After things got bad during the famine, Jacob sent Joseph's brothers down to Egypt to buy grain. When Joseph heard that his brothers were in town to buy grain, Joseph disguised himself and met with his brothers who wanted to buy enough grain to feed their families. When Joseph met them, the brothers bowed down to Joseph just as Joseph had dreamed prior to being sold into slavery. Instead of seeking revenge as he could have easily done, because by then Joseph was almost completely in charge of Egypt, Joseph instead showed mercy. Joseph's mercy restored the family.

In Matthew 5:7 Jesus taught His disciples that "Blessed are the merciful, for they shall be shown mercy." An attitude of being merciful is consistent with a person that has great faith. Some say that without mercy a person, even if he claims to be a Christian, is not worthy of the calling of God. Also, Jesus in the Model Prayer, said to pray that we will be forgiven our trespasses as we forgive the trespasses of those that trespass against us. Meaning that in forgiving we take on the forgiving nature of God, and we show great faith by acknowledging God's constant protection even in the face of those who may want to destroy us.

Moses Endured (Insults and all kinds of evil)

The children of Israel moved from Canaan to Egypt while Joseph was in charge. After the children of Israel began to multiply in numbers, another Pharaoh, not the one whose dream Joseph interpreted, became frightened by the number of Israelites in his country, Egypt. The descendants of Jacob became slaves in the land of Egypt because the new Pharaoh forgot all about Joseph and the contributions that the Israelites had made to Egypt. After 400 years of slavery the Israelites prayed for a savior that would take them out of bondage.

Meanwhile, an even more recent Pharaoh became even more paranoid and ordered that all newly born male children of the Israelites should be killed. Into that crisis, Moses was born. Moses' parents hid him for three months after he was born because they saw that he was no ordinary person even from birth and they were not afraid of violating Pharaoh's edict.

After hiding Moses for three months Moses family decided that they would build a small boat out of reeds and put the boat at a place where Pharaoh's daughter would be sure to find the boat with the child in it. Moses's sister, Miriam kept watch close by the boat. Sure enough, Pharaoh's daughter saw Moses and immediately fell in love with the child. Because Miriam was close by, she convinced Pharaoh's daughter that she knew someone who could take care of Moses until he was old enough to be weaned. Guess who Miriam chose to be Moses's nanny. You guessed it; Moses's mother was hired by Pharaoh's daughter to be Moses's nurse.

Moses's parents plan worked, and he was saved. Moses grew up in Pharaoh's house, was well educated, and everything seemed to be going in the right direction for Moses. One day however, Moses encountered a confrontation between one of the Pharaoh's men and one of the Hebrew slaves. In a fit of rage Moses killed Pharaoh's guy and was banished to the wilderness.

Moses wound up working for a man by the name of Jethro. Moses was hired to be a shepherd.

Moses had been so occupied for a considerable length of time, when one day while he was out in the back 40, he saw a peculiar site. There was a bush on fire, but it did not seem to be consumed by the fire.

Being a curious kind of person, Moses turned aside to see this site. As he approached Moses had his Damascus Road experience. From out of the burning bush the Lord spoke to Moses. Moses did not know who was speaking at first and asked, "Who are you." "I am that I am" was the reply. The Lord told Moses that he was going to become the savior of his people by leading them out of bondage.

Moses was reluctant at first, but the Lord insisted, and "Moses went down to Egypt's land and told old Pharaoh to let my people go." After God rained down plagues on the Egyptians the Pharaoh finally relented and Moses and the children of Israel set out for the Promised Land. Before they could get very far down the road Pharaoh changed his mind and he and his army came after the children of Israel.

The children of Israel were camped at the edge of the Red Sea and Pharaoh's army was closing in. Just when you thought all was lost, the Lord told Moses to raise up his staff and the Lord parted the waters of the Red Sea so that the Israelites could cross over on dry land. When the Egyptian army tried to follow, the waters closed over them, and they all drowned.

You would think that the Hebrew people after having witnessed these amazing events would be totally convinced that God was on their side and able to take care of all their needs and that all would go smoothly thereafter. That was not the case, however.

Soon the people's food began to run out and there was a scarcity of water in the Negev desert. The Hebrews started to blame Moses for their predicament. Miraculously, God provided manna for them to eat and freshwater for them to drink.

God called Moses to come up to Mount Sinai and to meet personally. God provided The Ten Commandments on stone tablets for the Israelites to live by. Moses had been meeting with God to receive the Ten Commandments for a lengthy period of time and while he was gone the people decided that they would build an idol of a golden calf and that would be their god. As a result, when Moses finally came down from Mount Sinai, he threw the tablets on which the Ten Commandments were written at the people and many of the people died.

God required that the people decide whether they were going to follow the true God or whether they were going to worship idols. After all, the second commandment says that "Thou shall not have any graven image." It seemed that the children of Israel were not ready for the Promise Land at that moment, so they wound up wondering in the desert for 40 years. When all those that had come out of the land of Egypt and crossed through the Red Sea on dry ground had passed away the Israelites were on the brink of crossing into the Promise Land. Moses leadership had been completed and God would not allow Moses to enter the Promise Land.

It seemed as if the children of Israel were continuously grumbling about Moses leadership and often caused Moses to suffer an immense pain in the neck. In Matthew 5:11 Jesus tells his disciples, "Blessed are you when people insult you, persecute you and falsely say all kinds of evil against you because of me. Rejoice and be glad, because great is your award in heaven, for in the same way they persecuted the prophets who were before you."

Moses suffered because it seemed as if every time he turned around, the people that he led out of slavery were complaining, insulting him, and saying all kinds of false things about him. On the other hand, Moses persevered. Moses' relationship with God never faltered and despite what people said about him Moses always remained faithful. One of the attributes of a person with great faith is that he/she can overcome the insults and persecutions of those who do not have the faith that is necessary to accomplish the goals that God has set out.

Jesus at John 15 :18 tells his disciples that, "If the world hates you keep in mind that it hated me first. If you belong to the world, it would love you as its own. As it is, you do not belong to the world, but I have chosen you out of the world. That is why the world hates you. Remember what I told you: 'A servant is not greater than his master.' If they persecuted me, they will persecute you also... whoever hates me hates my father as well. If I had not done among them the works no one else did, they would not be guilty of sin. As it is, they have seen, and yet they have hated me and my father. But this is to fulfill what is written in the law. They hated me without reason."

Do you ever feel that you are persecuted for no reason? Is it not interesting that Jesus told His disciples that we would be persecuted for no apparent reason? It is a measure of great faith when we are able to withstand the hatred of the world because of our stand with Jesus.

The Beatitudes

If you have not noticed by now, I have equated each of the above referenced individuals, starting with Abel and going through Moses with one of the Beatitudes stated by Jesus in the Sermon on the Mount. I am convinced that the commands of Jesus are the most essential part of gaining great faith. The traits of a person with great faith are; first, a total reliance on the sufficiency of God also referred to as godliness; secondly, a sense of humility because we are aware of our own sinful nature and shortcomings; thirdly, a willingness to be subject to the instruction of God sometimes referred to as meekness; fourthly, a diligence in seeking God's will in our lives, that is like a person who hungers and thirsts after righteousness; fifthly the ability to show mercy even when it is very difficult; sixthly, a heart that is pure; seventhly, a willingness to bring peace into any situation; eighthly, the ability to withstand persecution and insult when you are sure you are in God's protective will.

Chapter 3
Living the Adventure

Availability

Some people respond to a Damascus Road experience in a positive and meaningful way while others may not even know that they are having a Damascus Road experience. Going back to Paul's experience, I am sure that when he set out for Damascus on the day that he met Jesus on that road that he did not expect that his life would change so dramatically. Paul probably got up and washed his face. He put on his shoes and started up the road. Paul was walking perhaps talking to his companions and not thinking that the Lord was getting ready to intervene in his life, when he was blinded and heard the voice of Jesus demanding to know why Paul was persecuting Jesus's followers and therefore persecuting Jesus himself. The only thing Paul could do was to ask, "Who are you?"

If such an event as Paul experienced on the road to Damascus occurred in my life, I am not sure how I would respond. Perhaps it would depend on what I was doing at the time, where I was going, who I was with, and whether I was available to understand what was happening. Availability is a key ingredient to our response to a Damascus Road experience. Availability means that we are conscious, expectant, seeking, prepared, curious, trusting, and willing to engage by faith in the great adventure to which we are being called. Such an event happened to me when I was 10 years old. I heard the call of Jesus to surrender my life to Him. I have never regrated my decision to follow Jesus and believe it is the most significant and meaningful decision that I have ever made.

I call the response to a Damascus Road experience a great adventure because if we are responding to God's call in our lives, we are destined for the assurance that we are following God's will. We will be called to start on an adventure that may take us to places that we would least expect and allow us to participate in the lives of others who are called for God's purposes. While I am not sure how Paul felt when he was struck down that fateful day, the adventures that are told about Paul's life in Acts and even in Paul's correspondence tell of his total reliance on God and depicts a life full of adventure. That adventurous life is evident in the events that he describes in his letters to the various churches that he ministered to during his life.

Consciousness

In order to realize that we have been called to perform God's will, we must be conscious. Ancient and more modern thought regarding the levels of consciousness evoke physical, emotional, and spiritual platforms. We all think of ourselves as being aware of the internal and external stimuli to which we must respond in order to live on a daily basis. We are conscious that the night has ended, and it is time to get up and go to work. Our internal clocks tell us we are getting hungry, and it is time to find something to eat. We are conscious of the hunger pangs. From an emotional standpoint we are consciously aware of when people are making fun of us, we are conscious of insults, flirtations, that someone is hitting on me or that because she is so pretty that I want to hit on her. We feel love, anger, joy and sadness. From a spiritual standpoint our level of consciousness may not be so easily described and there is much speculation about the spiritual realm that may lead us into very divergent areas of thought.

In ancient cultures the search for reasons for everything as a basis for cultural understanding, developed. We do not know when mankind first developed its awareness of spiritual consciousness, but we do know that in ancient societies there seemed to be a search for understanding of why we as humans become aware that each of us has a distinct personality. Some writers contend that ancient civilization's search for reasons for human existence, for everything as a basis of cultural understanding, developed approximately 102,000 years ago.

The concept of right and wrong developed in humans that led to a progressive awareness and concern for others. There are theories of human cognitive development that take into consideration the evolution of the human brain's capacity for thought. (See Jean Piaget) More modern neurological research delves into the brain's capacity for spontaneity, calculation, and creativity. As mentioned above E.O. Wilson in The Meaning of Human Existence, indicates that evolutionary processes have caused the brain to be hardwired for certain thought patterns and that there are also portions of the human brain that are soft wired and can be easily changed by conscious thought.

Sigmund Freud conceptualized three facets of the psychic apparatus. He described the "id" as that portion of the consciousness that is primal. The id is present at birth. It consists of unconscious instincts and primitive behaviors. While it is the source of psychic energy it is the primary component of personality. The desire for pleasure is the overwhelming driving force of the id but can also produce senses of anxiety or tension.

The "ego," according to Freud, causes individuals to deal with reality. Because of the ego, the impulses of the id can be expressed in a manner acceptable in the real world. The ego is expressed in consciousness, pre-consciousness and the unconscious mind. The ego weighs the costs and benefits of satisfying human desires.

Internalized moral standards are expressed according to Freud in the "superego." The superego expresses ideals and separates right from wrong. The superego causes us to understand the behavior patterns given to us by our parents and by society. From the superego we obtain feelings of guilt and remorse. The three facets of the psychic apparatus according to Freud, cannot be separated but act together dynamically to produce human personality and moderate human behavior. Human personality, as described by Freud, is but one description of complex human behavior and the levels of consciousness.

From a psychological standpoint our beliefs, prejudices, levels of acceptance of ideas and personalities can be explained by functions of the brain. Study of the brain has led to mapping sections of the brain that relate to specific functions. Neurologists have studied the impact of hormones and chemical balances that can cause mental illness if the hormones and chemical balances are out of order.

None of this however explains the influence of God in any individual's life nor does it explain each individual's desire to believe that there is a God, and that God has something to do with me. Judeo-Christian thought brings an aspect of spirituality to human consciousness. From that standpoint, "In the beginning there was God." God created. God created men and women. "Then God said let us make man in our own image after our own likeness... So, God created mankind in His own image, in the image of God He created them male and female He created them." Genesis 1:26-27.

As a result of this creative process the Bible tells us that the image of God was imbedded into all humankind. From the beginning, according to Christian thought, a desire to have a relationship with God is a part of being human. (Atheists disagree of course) How a relationship with God translates itself into human personality is the cause of much discussion and divergence of thought. However, there seems to be uniformity within Christianity that we are created by God and that a relationship with God is a matter of a conscious desire on our part and on the part of God. Christians believe that God exists, and that God has a role for us in this life. Christianity has been the major influence on the development of Western Civilization. Paul's influence on the development of Christian thought cannot be diminished.

Because there is a God, He must want something from me. I think that that axiom deserves some explanation. When Paul got up on the morning when Jesus confronted him, he believed that he was carrying out what God wanted him to do, but he was going in the exact wrong direction. At the exact moment that he was confronted by Jesus, Paul became conscious of a direction that caused him not only to change his name but also to change his opinion about what God would have him do with his life. If we believe that there is a God, then we must also come to the realization that God is in control and in particular that God is in control of me. When Paul was on the road to Damascus It suddenly occurred to Paul that God was going to change the direction in which Paul was going. When I become aware of God's direction in my life, that revelation is often referred to as submitting to God's will.

God has created me to be a social being. I desire relationships because God himself desires a relationship with me. Jesus' desire was for Paul to stop doing what he was doing and change directions. Paul consciously accepted God's change of direction in his life. If Paul was an atheist or was not conscious of God's call on his life either someone else would have had to step up to do what God wanted or Western Civilization may not have evolved in the way that it did.

Therefore, a conscious awareness that God has created me and that he wants a relationship with me allows me to seek God's will. If I am open to this conscious awareness (by its very nature conscious awareness requires openness on my part) then I am in a position to respond positively to any Damascus Road experience that I may encounter.

Expectation

Am I expecting that I will encounter God as I go about my daily life? Living a life in which we are expecting a message from God is important to every modern-day Christian. Too often we live a life in which we do not expect to have a direct message from God. We may even read our Bible on a daily basis and not expect a revelation from Scripture. On the other hand, Jesus tells us to "Seek ye first the kingdom of God and His righteousness and all these things will be added unto you." Matthew 6:33. Additionally Jesus tells us to ask, knock, and seek because if we ask it will be given, if we knock it shall be opened, and if we seek, we shall find. Living a life of expectation that we will hear a direct message from our Lord is important because we never want to miss an opportunity to live out God's will in our own lives.

There is a big difference between expectation and anxiety. An expectation is a belief that we are about to receive that for which we have been waiting. Anxiety, on the other hand, is an emotional state in which we are in dread of what may or may not happen. I expect that God will reveal his plan for my life at the time that I need that information and that encouragement. How do we go from anxiety to expectation?

In Matthew 6: 24-34 Jesus informs us that there is no need to be anxious about what we eat, drink or wear. Jesus tells us that God knows what we need and that he will supply our needs. The greater question is not our physical needs but our need to come into the kingdom of God and His righteousness. Jesus states that our prayer should include a desire that our Father's kingdom will come. After all, the whole purpose of a Damascus Road experience is so that God's kingdom will be exposed to those that accept the call of Jesus in their lives. Again, in Philippians 4:6-7 the apostle Paul after he had been changed by his Damascus Road experience states, "The Lord is near, do not be anxious about anything but in every situation by prayer and petition with Thanksgiving, present your requests to God and the peace of God that passes all understanding will guard your hearts and mind in Christ Jesus."

The expectancy of a Damascus Road experience in our own personal lives allows us to change from a life in which we are anxious about our daily needs to a life in which we are yearning for the nearness of the Lord so that His kingdom will be exposed to anyone who is willing to repent, accept Jesus as their Savior, take up their cross and follow Him.

Seeking

"Seek and you shall find." What are we to search for and how do we know when we have found it? Of course, the obvious answer is we are to search for the kingdom of God and His righteousness. The first stage of that search is self-examination. Both Jesus and John the Baptist told those that were listening, to repent. In order to repent we must examine our old self. This examination must occur often if we truly want to know what God wants from us.

Self-examination requires that we pray that God will show us our personality defects, habits that need to be changed, attitudes that need to be adjusted, and unconfessed sins. This can be quite an undertaking especially if it has been a long time since we have last examined our spiritual selves. By seeking to know my own shortcomings and to commit to making proper changes I have taken the first step towards seeking God's kingdom and His righteousness. Righteousness is a state of being in which I have become more and more godly. Remember Abel. God considered him righteous because he had the right attitude when it came to making a sacrificial offering. The difference between Abel and Cain was that Abel's attitude was correct as opposed to his brothers.

The second step in seeking the kingdom of God and His righteousness is to fill our lives with godliness. Asking for a greater filling of the Holy Spirit produces a greater closeness with God's kingdom.

Filling oneself with the Holy Spirit requires a belief that God will fulfill the request that we make. On the other hand, it is important that our request for a greater filling of the Holy Spirit is made sincerely and for the right motives. God wants our attention. We need God's closeness. A proper attitude and a diligent seeking are necessary.

We must always be aware of those who would abuse the name of God for personal satisfaction. So-called ministers of the gospel that use their power of influence for personal gain, wealth, power, impure interests, and are risking God's admonition to not use His name in vain. Jesus tells us in the Sermon on the Mount, that when you give alms (tithes and offerings and money to the church) that you should do it in secret so that only our Father in heaven will know what we have given. Preachers who continually beg for money from their congregations and who require public demonstrations of offerings from the people in the pews, have violated a very important spiritual concept. Jesus told his followers that they should store up treasures in heaven were neither moth nor rust corrupt nor thieves break in and steal. Beware of those who preach the prosperity gospel for as Jesus says their reward has already occurred and their reward is not in heaven.

We are not to seek money. We are to seek spiritual gifts. Those gifts according to Paul in 1 Corinthians 12:7-11 include, "A manifestation of the Spirit is given to each person for the common good. To one is given a message of wisdom through the Spirit, to another, a message of knowledge by the same spirit, to another faith by the same Spirit, to another, gifts of healing by the one Spirit, to another the performing of miracles, to another prophecy, to another distinguishing between spirits, to another different kinds of tongues, to another interpretation of tongues. One and the same spirit is active in all these, distributing to each person as He wills." Having a spiritual gift of wisdom or knowledge or of any of the other spiritual gifts listed above, bring rewards in heaven and are not subject to corruption. Seeking spiritual gifts is important. Taking on the lifestyle of the rich and famous is an abomination. If we seek that which is pure and holy, we are prone to be seeking that which Jesus offers and that puts us in a position to live a righteous life in the kingdom of God. When we are seeking the manifestations of the spirit, we have opened ourselves to a Damascus Road experience.

Preparation

Jesus tells his disciples that a person does not build a house without considering the foundation on which he is building. Nor does a King go to war without knowing the army against whom he is fighting. In other words, if we are going to attempt to build a building or fight a war we need to be prepared. Preparation is a key ingredient in determining and following God's plan for my life. Preparation requires training and discipline of thought as well as actions.

Every athlete knows that he must practice in order to be prepared to perform at his/her best when the contest is on the line. A football player develops his skills by constantly working out, getting stronger, and knowing the proper position in which to be when the play starts. To be successful the football player must understand his opponent's strengths and weaknesses and commit himself to victory.

Paul also believed that preparation was a necessary component of the spiritual life. In 1st Corinthians 9:24- 26 Paul writes, "Do you not know that in a race all the runners run, but only one gets the prize? Run in such a way as to get the prize. Everyone who competes in the games goes into strict training. They do it to get a crown that will not last, but we do it to get a crown that will last forever. Therefore, I do not run like someone running aimlessly; I do not fight like a boxer beating the air." Evidently running and boxing were the sporting events of the day rather than football. The point, however, is that just like an athlete every Christian must go into strict training in order to achieve victory.

Self-discipline requires that we control our thoughts as well as our actions. In 2 Timothy 4 after telling Timothy that the day will come when people will not put up with sound doctrine and, instead to suit their own desires, will gather around them a great number of teachers to say what their itching ears want to hear, Paul announces that believer's minds will wonder from the instructions that they have received from Paul and from Jesus himself. Paul then at verse 6 talks about his own demise. "For I am already being poured out like a drink offering, my time for departure is near." But in verse 7 he tells Timothy the key to victory and says, "I have fought the good fight I have finished the race I have kept the faith." Therefore, Paul is warning Timothy that at some point in the future even believers will stray from the sound teachings of Christ. They will want to hear and believe that religion is like a talisman, a good luck charm, which can be manipulated to fulfill their own self desires. On the other hand, Paul admonishes Timothy to keep the faith and to fight the good fight and to finish the race that is set before him. Faith is the key to victory. The purposeful study of the Bible is necessary to keep our hearts and minds on the prize. Purposeful study begins with a prayerful attitude in which I seek the Holy Spirits guidance in seeking the truth of the passage I am studying.

Additionally, the writer of Hebrews tells us at 12:1, "Therefore, since we are surrounded by such a great cloud of witnesses, let us throw off everything that hinders and the sin that so easily entangles. Let us run with perseverance the race marked out for us, fixing our eyes on Jesus, the pioneer and perfecter of faith." We must keep our eyes on Jesus. If we do that, we can do no wrong and we will always be prepared for the conflicts that will inevitably come our way.

While we train to control our own thoughts and desires by focusing on our faith in Jesus, it is also necessary for us to consider the fight that we are subjecting ourselves to when we become Christians. In Ephesians 6 we are told to "Put on the whole armor of God, so that you may be able to stand against the wiles of the devil. We do not wrestle against flesh and blood, but against principalities, against powers, against the rulers of the darkness of the world, against spiritual wickedness in high places."

The devil is an active entity that is constantly on the prowl to devour those who believe and especially those who are not committed to Christ Jesus. In the Lord's Prayer Jesus tells us to pray that we will be delivered from evil (Matthew 6:15). It is necessary to be delivered from evil because evil is all around us and seeks to destroy us. Only by the power of God can we be spared from the destruction that evil causes.

In the Screwtape Letters, C.S. Lewis provides his view of how a group of the devil's minions go about victimizing people who are unaware. In Genesis (the first book of the Bible), Satan is depicted as the most subtle of creatures. It has been said that Satan is the father of all lies. People who habitually lie are so influenced by evil that they cannot distinguish reality and truth because of the influence of evil. We must be careful not to be caught up in lies. In the 10 Commandments we are told that we should not bear false witness. (Exodus 20:16)

One of the attributes of a Spirit filled life is that we are given discernment in order to separate truth from lies. If we have not put on the armor of God so that we can stand against the wiles of the devil it is imperative that we undertake God's protection as quickly as possible. We should immerse ourselves in the Scriptures and ask the Holy Spirit to lead us to the truth that is contained in God's word.

We measure truth by whether it is uplifting, "Finally, brothers and sisters, whatever is true, whatever is honorable, whatever is right, whatever is pure, whatever is lovely, whatever is commendable-if anything is excellent or praiseworthy-think about such things." Philippians 4:8. If we fill our minds and spirits with what is good there is no room for lies or the evil that accompanies lies and those who lie. As I have previously related there is no evil in God, and Jesus lived a perfectly pure life. There is no deceit with God. God does not try to trick us or defraud us. Therefore, if we are going to live godly lives, we must also be people who are true to our word and who do not seek to deceive. Today's culture is full of people who seek to deceive. We must guard ourselves so that we do not fall into the temptation of seeking to deceive.

Truth does not seek to convince us that we are in need. Truth does not try to convince us that we do not have what everybody else has. It is the way of the world to convince us that we are unworthy and that by accepting unrealistic promises that our lives will be enriched. Paul states in Ephesians 6:14 that we are to stand firm with a belt of truth fastened securely around our waist. In that metaphor Paul tells us that it is essential that everything be bound together with truth. A Roman soldier needed a heavy belt in which to carry his sword, and the other implements necessary in order to protect himself and to carry out his duties as a soldier. In Paul's mind, truth was so essential that everything else was connected to it.

Paul goes on to say that we are to put on the breastplate of righteousness. The belt of truth held the breastplate of righteousness in place. Righteousness is an identifying factor of those that belong to Christ. The breastplate of the Roman soldier contained the emblems of the Army for which the soldier was fighting. It was the means by which other soldiers identified each other. The same is true of Christians; we identify each other by the truth that we stand for and the righteousness to which we adhere.

Because Satan is very subtle many times half-truths and things that seem to be alluring, desirable, and worthwhile may turn out to be lies. We are to guard ourselves by insisting on the truth in order to overcome the evil that is around us. When we have sufficiently girded ourselves with truth and righteousness, we will be prepared not only to receive a Damascus Road experience but also to ward off the evil that is always around us.

Curiosity

Curiosity may have killed the cat but without it we might be still living in caves without fire. Because of curiosity we have developed smart phones, have walked on the moon, can watch live sporting events that are occurring on the other side of the world, and fill ourselves with junk food that will eventually kill us. Mankind has always been curious about our relationship with God. Humans from the earliest recorded times have wanted to know about God. Religious practices have been evident in the most primitive societies. As humans we want to know what God wants of us. We are curious about not only if there is a God but what it is that God requires.

Fake religion

Who does not remember Jim Jones and the people that drank the poison Kool-Aid in Guyana? How can we forget David Koresh and the Davidian Temple in Waco, Texas where women and children were burned to death? I have already spoken about the prosperity gospel above. It seems that every day a new religion is started. Many of these new religions are not based on anything but the personality of the man or woman who claims to be the messenger of God. Perhaps these men and women are sincere but on the other hand maybe they are not. Why are we subject to being caught up in fake religions, and how can we determine the difference between what is true and what is fake?

We as Christians, especially Christians living in the United States, where freedom of religion is guaranteed in the First Amendment to the United States Constitution, must be constantly on guard to discern truth from the lies that so easily surround us. Paul, Peter and John in their letters to the churches in Europe and in Asia Minor on many occasions warned Christians to be on guard of false teachings and religions that seem to be in accordance with the teachings of Jesus but varied either significantly or slightly from His commandments. Further, as in the motion picture, Elmer Gantry what may start out to be based on biblical principles can turn into a religion that is no more than a personality cult.

Being fooled and temptation to believe

We as humans want to sincerely believe that we have come to the right conclusion concerning what is good for us and are willing to stake our beliefs on representation made (often times) by strangers. After all, advertising seeks to convince us that the product that Madison Avenue is selling is something that we must have or that our lives will be diminished if we do not have that new product. Because we want to believe, we can and at times do become the victim of a scheme to deprive us of our money. People who commit the crime of fraud, pray on those who want to believe what oftentimes would be impossible to comprehend. After all, how many times has a slick salesman sold swamp property in Florida or an interest in the Brooklyn Bridge?

On the other hand, because fraud by its very nature is subtle, often we can be convinced by representations and assertions by people who appear to be in a superior position and who by their persuasiveness causes us to rely on and believe that what we are being told or sold is for our own good. I have many years of experience in handling cases in court involving fraud. I have seen lives destroyed by those that would take advantage of others. Misleading representations, designed to cause consumers to rely on those assertions, are found in most advertising campaigns. We are all subject to being misled. By our very nature we want to believe. What is it that makes us people who are subject to being caught up in schemes that seek to persuade us to believe in something that is not in our best interests? Unfortunately, the elderly are most often the targets of con artists.

We who are raised by parents and are taught from the time we are infants to rely on those who have authority over us can also be susceptible to perpetrators of fraud. When we are babies, we cry, and our mothers stop what they are doing and feed us. When we are uncomfortable mother changes our diapers. Therefore, from an early age we are subject to believing that our needs will be met by those who have authority over us.

We do not give up our reliance on our parents until we reach adolescence when we begin to rebel as a natural part of maturity. Some of us never lose our reliance on those who appear to have authority over us. Others of us, even though we have reached a level of maturity tend to rely on authority figures to lead us. There are psychological studies in which tolerance for authority can be measured by personality type. The ability to discern whether we are being misled, only comes when we have reached a level of maturity that allows us to evaluate representations not solely on the basis of the authority figure making the representation, but on an evaluation of the factual basis on which the representation is made.

Christians must be constantly on guard concerning false teachings. The New Testament is full of warnings about wolves in sheep's clothing that would deceive believers. As stated above, because the devil is subtle slight variations in the basic truths of the Christian faith can lead us away from the commands of our Lord. In the Sunday school class that I teach, we are constantly having a discussion concerning whether there are absolutes within our faith to which we must adhere. Some in my class take the position that everything is relative and that there are really no absolutes. I disagree with the latter proposition. It is our duty as Christians to take hold of the absolute truths that are provided to us in the Gospels and rely on those truths even though others would vary the absolute truth of the gospel to suit their own needs. It is my belief that we must search diligently through the Scriptures in order to understand and come to the truth by which God would have us to live.

Discernment

It is critically important to modern-day Christians to have a better understanding of the teachings of Jesus Christ. I suggest that Christians study the Sermon on the Mount (Matthew 5 through 7 and corresponding passages in Luke) on a regular basis. Even memorization of those portions of the New Testament would be helpful. If we are going to be Christians, we should strive to understand the words of our Lord that were given to us as the basis of our faith. Holding up any representation made to us in light of the teachings of Jesus is a good first step in determining whether the representation being made is reliable and profitable to us.

If we consider the teachings of those who espouse the prosperity gospel as opposed to the words of Jesus teachings regarding money and the temptation to serve money, we come to a very different conclusion about the place of materialism in the lives of Christians. Jesus made it plain that we could not serve money and God. Because materialism is so rampant, especially in the United States and Western Europe, it would appear that the influence of materialism has replaced Jesus' admonition that one cannot serve God and money at the same time. (Matthew 6: 24) Additionally, the first of the 10 Commandments requires that we have no other God than the Lord God. Thus, we are to submit first to God and rely on God's grace rather than on our wealth as the basis of our faith. This is but one portion of the teachings of Jesus that must be understood before we can properly evaluate those that seem to be speaking with absolute authority.

Humility

Another important part of Jesus teachings was the place of humility in our lives. While Jesus had authority over every aspect of nature (he calmed the winds with a single command, changed water into wine, and even walked on water), He was able to speak with authority even with those who supposedly had more education (when Jesus was 12 years old, He amazed the rulers of the temple in Jerusalem and spoke with authority to those who heard Him teach; Luke 2: 41-52). Even when Jesus exercised His authority over demons (He often commanded evil spirits to vacate fragile humans) He did so with great humility.

In the Sermon on the Mount Jesus cautioned those who wished to call attention to themselves. He said that those praying in public, those giving alms, and even those who were fasting, should do so in secret so that only God would hear, see or have knowledge of those essential parts of one's faith. While it is somewhat a part of human nature to want to call attention to our good deeds, it is more essential that we perform our obligations to God so that only God knows, because He always knows our intentions anyway. We must be humble. Jesus was humble. He could have had anything that he desired but chose to submit Himself to the cross in an act of complete humility and sacrifice. If that is the attitude of Christ let it also be my attitude!

Anxiety

Jesus also admonished us not to be anxious or to worry about own needs. He instructed us to consider the birds of the air and flowers. Birds neither sow nor reap nor have barns to keep their stuff in, but God sees their needs and takes care of them. Jesus tells us that not even Solomon, perhaps the richest man ever to live, could match the beauty of the wildflowers that grow without anyone tending to them. Thus, we too should not be concerned with what we put on, because God looks into our hearts not at our clothes.

The Golden Rule

Lastly, not only are we to treat others with great respect, but we are also to go out of our way in order to see the needs of others and to respond in a way that we would expect others to respond to our needs. Perhaps the high point of the Sermon on the Mount (Matthew 7: 12) is what is referred to as the Golden Rule.

There Jesus goes much beyond the common practice of not interfering with someone's well-being; but Jesus requires us to "do unto others as you would have them do unto you." This single phrase may be the high point of Jesus teachings. When you begin to think about the ramifications of doing onto others, it takes away our tendency to be greedy, self-absorbed, neglectful, narcissistic, rude and honorary. On the other hand, when we take into consideration the other man's needs and act on them, we tend to be humble, helpful, compassionate and godly. If we are able to provide for the other man's needs, we are truly living in God's image because that is how He treats us. I pray that this is how I live my life. Jesus also said that everyone would know that we are Christians by our love for one another. Because Jesus loves me, I must also be identified by my love for you.

The words of Jesus are unique, satisfying, urgent, and necessary especially in the world in which we live. Before Jesus ascended into heaven, He told His closest disciples that He would send a comforter to be with them, instruct them, and provide direction for every circumstance of their life. That same comforter, the Holy Spirit, is present in the lives of Christians today. The fact that there is a Holy Spirit that Christians can access is a difference maker when it comes to going from someone that has little faith to becoming a person of great faith.

Access to the Holy Spirit

Access to the Holy Spirit makes Christianity different from all the other major religions. The difference being that we carry within us the power of God, the direction of God, and the very being of

God. When Jesus told His disciples that He was going to prepare a place for them and that He would come again, He also told them that He would send an advocate, a counselor, a comforter, the Holy Spirit to provide them with direction for their lives. John 16:7. Paul tells us that when we are saved that we are sealed by the Holy Spirit. Paul also tells us that it is possible to grieve the Holy Spirit so that our access to the power that the Holy Spirit provides to us may become diminished. Therefore, we as Christians need to seek fuller access to the Holy Spirit in order to gain an increased measure of faith.

How then do we seek a fuller measure of the presence of the Holy Spirit in our lives? Some communities of belief within Christianity, believe that we are to seek a second baptism in which we gain access and an empowerment of the Holy Spirit. I have had the experience of worshiping with members of the Full Gospel community of believers. It is their practice to ask the Holy Spirit into their lives separately from their salvation experience. In that way, members of that community of belief, gain spiritual abilities usually manifested by ecstatic speaking otherwise known as speaking in tongues. While I do not doubt the sincerity of that faith community, I do not believe it is necessary to seek a second baptism. I do however believe that it is important to always seek a fuller measure of the presence of the Holy Spirit in our lives.

Jesus tells us at Matthew 7:7-8 and Luke 11:9 that "Ask, and it should be given to you; seek, and ye shall find; knock and it shall be opened unto you. For everyone that asks, receives; and he that seeks finds; and to him that knocks it shall be opened." There may be a problem if we are not constantly asking, seeking and knocking. My reading of the Bible tells me that God honors those that diligently seek Him and are constantly driven by a desire to have a closer and fuller relationship with Him. Honestly, there are times when I feel the presence of the Holy Spirit in my life in a more intimate relationship than at other times. I am aware that as a Christian that my life has been bought with a very high price and that it is incumbent on me to be responsive to the presence of the Holy Spirit by seeking to live a godlier life. Further, my prayer life needs to take into consideration the yearning of the spirit within me to reach out for a fuller measure of God's presence.

What happens to us when we do not sufficiently ask, seek, or knock? We wind up in a perpetual state of stagnant inertia. As we discussed earlier inertia requires an outside force to cause us to change the direction and the velocity of our spiritual lives. The force that overcomes spiritual inertia is in fact the Holy Spirit within us that allows us to be directed by God. Once we seek a closer relationship with God, the Holy Spirit empowers us to find the direction that God has chosen for us.

The other night I was listening to Charles Stanley preaching on his In Touch television program. Pastor Stanley stated that the Holy Spirit, if we allow it, can be in constant communication with Christians directing their activities. Stanley stated that when you feel that whatever activity you are about to embark on is not right, it is the Holy Spirit speaking to you and directing your activity. The Holy Spirit, however, not only blocks negative activities but also can cause us to move in the direction that God has appointed for us. Perhaps it is the call to action that is the most difficult portion of the Holy Spirit's presence for us to comprehend. Again, inertia can prevent us from taking the action that we need to take if we are to act in accordance with God's will. After all Newton observed the objects at rest tend to stay at rest. If your spiritual life is not progressing and dynamic, perhaps it is because you are not asking the Holy Spirit to get you off the bench and get you back in the game.

When we discussed the honor roll of those who have great faith, it was evident that each one of the commended individuals acted on God's direction to step out in faith. In other words, none of those mentioned in Hebrews: 11 were couch potatoes, no one stayed home to watch football on TV, not one of those individuals was a skeptic or non-believer. Each of the commended heard God's call and acted on the belief that God's Spirit would see them through. Therefore, because we have access to the Holy Spirit, and because the Holy Spirit directs us in both negative and positive ways, it is necessary for us to attune ourselves to the directions that we are given.

Spiritual Gifts

Paul tells us that each of us is given spiritual gifts. In Romans 12:4-6 Paul states: "... each of us has one body with many members, and these members do not all have the same function, so in Christ we who are many from one body, and each member belongs to all others. We have different gifts according to the grace given to us." In Romans 12 the list of spiritual gifts includes: exhortation, giving, leadership, mercy, prophecy, service, and teaching. In 1 Corinthians 12 Paul's list includes: administration, apostles, discernment, faith, healings, helps, knowledge and miracles. The list also states that some are given to be prophets, teachers and some will have the ability to speak in tongues and interpret ecclesiastic speech. In that list there is also the gift of wisdom. In Ephesians 4 the list of spiritual gifts includes: apostle, evangelism, pastor, prophecy and teacher. Scattered throughout the New Testament are references to the gifts of celibacy, hospitality, martyrdom, missionary service and voluntary poverty. Each of the gifts listed has relevance to the service of the Christian in order to announce and strengthen the kingdom of God.

As you can see there is a wide variety of gifts given to Christians. A few years ago, there was a great emphasis on trying to find out what your spiritual gift was and how to use that gift. I personally have been a Sunday school teacher for over 40 years and am convinced that teaching is my spiritual gift. Because I am certain that I am called to be a teacher of the Gospel of Christ, does that mean that there are other spiritual gifts that are available to me that I should use or that would be beneficial to God's kingdom?

The answer may lie in determining the spiritual need that is present at the time that we are called upon for our service. There may be times when it is necessary for me to engage in evangelism. In fact, I have been called on to act as an evangelist and have been very comfortable with that role. Many years ago, I was asked to be a member of a group of individuals from different parts of Georgia to conduct evangelistic events throughout Georgia. We conducted lay lead revivals on weekends at churches that invited us to train church members in evangelism and to go to individual's homes that had been identified by the church members as being in need of salvation.

I experienced the movement of the Holy Spirit and was able to see results of the Holy Spirit's activity in the lives of complete strangers. At other times I have been called upon to engage in hospitality, giving of gifts, and other manifestations of the presence of the Holy Spirit. For these times and for the activity of the Holy Spirit in my life I am extremely grateful.

I am sure that each of us if we look back on our lives can see times when the Holy Spirit was active, and we felt the presence of God acting through us in meaningful ways.

Service

I know that you have heard it said if you do not use it, you lose it. Each of us is called upon to use the gifts that we have been given to enhance the Kingdom of God. One of the most poignant parables of our Lord is that of the talents. In that story the Master was taking a trip to a distant land, and he entrusted some of his fortune (a gift) to his servants. To one servant he gave five shares, to another two shares and lastly to another servant one share.

On the Masters return he required an accounting from his servants. From the one servant that he had given the five shares, the accounting was exceptionally good. While the Master was away this faithful servant invested the shares that he had been given and was able to make twice as much as he had been given. From the servant who had been given two shares again the report was very good. That servant was able to invest what he had been given and double the value. From the last servant to whom only one share was given the report was not so good. That servant told the Master that he was afraid to invest the share that he had been given and instead wrapped it in a cloth and buried it in the backyard.

When this account was given to the Master, the Master's, displeasure was readily apparent. The Master stripped that servant of all his shares, required that that servant's share be turned over to the servant to whom the five shares had been given and the servant that had buried that share was cast into the outer darkness where there will be weeping and gnashing of teeth. (Matthew 25:14-30).

Interestingly, in that parable Jesus says this in verse 29, "For to everyone who has will more be given, and he will have an abundance. But from the one who has not, even what he has will be taken away." As a cautionary warning please remember Jesus was speaking of spiritual matters and not of earthly treasure.

So, what does the story say to us? First it is clear that the Lord has blessed each of us with spiritual gifts. To some he gives greater gifts than others, but it is clear that he gives gifts to each of us. It is our duty to take an inventory of the gifts that we have received so that we will be able to use those gifts and to give an account of our use of those gifts. Further, when the gifts that you are given are utilized for the benefit of the Lord, you will receive the Lord's blessing and the gifts that He has given will be multiplied. The faithful servant will receive the joy of the Master's, blessing. On the other hand, if you fail to use the gifts that you are given you run the risk of the Master's, wrath. It is obvious that each of us would rather receive the Lord's blessing than fall victim to wasting the gifts the Lord has given us and His judgment.

As I have previously stated there are any number of gifts that can be entrusted to each of us for the furtherance of God's kingdom. I provided a list of the spiritual gifts that are included in Paul's letters to the churches, the list of gifts was not to be considered as the exclusive listing of all spiritual gifts that are available to be given by Jesus or to be used in service to God's kingdom. But the question remains, how do I know which gift has been given to me? The answer to that question should be obvious but it is not obvious to everyone.

For instance, I believe that I was given the gift to be a teacher. I did not recognize that I had the gift of teaching until I was called upon by someone at my church to start teaching young children. When I started teaching those children it was very difficult at first because I did not have any experience. Later, while I was attending Sunday school at my church, I was able to engage with those also in attendance in a meaningful way. Before long I was asked to teach an adult Sunday school class made up of people my own age. For the last 45 years I have engaged in teaching various Sunday school classes ranging from college students to the oldest ladies Sunday school class in my church. I have felt the calling of the Lord to continue to teach Sunday school classes and receive great joy and satisfaction from teaching those classes. During the time that I have been teaching Sunday school I also was called upon to join a group of men that engaged in personal evangelism throughout the state of Georgia. It was my complete joy to on occasions assist someone in making a commitment to Jesus Christ.

From what I have just said, you may think that understanding your spiritual gifts is somewhat haphazard. I hope that you do not consider my experience in trying to understand my spiritual gifts as being a hit or miss situation. However, I believe it is an openness to accept the calling of the Holy Spirit that is necessary. When we are open to the acceptance of a spiritual calling, the Holy Spirit will call upon us.

Early on, others recognized my ability to understand the Scripture and to effectively communicate my understanding to others. It is possible that I could have rejected the invitation to teach children when I was first called upon to do that. After all, at that time I had no children of my own and was more interested in pursuing my career and other activities. At one time in my life, I believe that I was a good enough athlete to become a professional baseball player. I could have pursued that adventure to a greater degree than I wound up doing. On the other hand, it was clear that teaching children and then teaching adults and engaging in personal evangelism were in furtherance of God's kingdom rather than my own personal happiness in playing baseball.

There has not been a time when my service in furtherance of the calling, that Jesus has placed on my life, has caused me to question whether I was putting the talent (spiritual gift) that I was given to use. Although sometimes I have felt that I was beating my head against the wall in trying to explain that what I was teaching was the true meaning of scripture to those who were my students. Nevertheless, I have continually felt the presence of the Holy Spirit when I have taught the Sunday school lesson on Sundays.

For many years Eva Trailer was a prayer partner of mine. We would meet in the prayer room at church every Sunday an hour before Sunday school. We would pray for the needs of the church and for each other. Eva at the time was 94 years old and had had a long history of service. Eva would prepare Wednesday night supper for the church. She and a friend of hers had a routine of planning the meals, doing the shopping, preparing the meals and then cleaning up after. Eva had the gift of hospitality, and everyone loved her service to the church. I asked Eva how she came to be the person responsible for Wednesday night meals at the church. She said she felt led to share her ability to plan and cook the meals. She stated that it was a gift that she had been given. My experience with Eva was that she was also gifted in her concern for the church through her daily prayer life. She also, on a regular basis, kept in touch with shut-ins that were church members and regularly called each of the members of her Sunday school class at least on a weekly basis in order to encourage them. It was clear that Eva knew what her abilities were and intended to maximize the use of her gifts.

You could say that Eva has the gift of service. Because we all have spiritual gifts, we are called upon to put those gifts into God's service because that is the calling to which each of us must strive in order to fulfill the call of Jesus on our lives. If we are not ready for service, we are not ready for our own personal Damascus Road experience.

Trusting

While we are to be deliberate and discerning regarding our spiritual gifts, and also wary of those who would try to distort our beliefs. There is also a necessity of trusting the Holy Spirit to allow us to be open to Jesus' call. Where do we find that to which we can trust in order to understand and appreciate the leadership of the Holy Spirit? I believe that the answer is found in a greater study of the Holy Scriptures.

A deliberate and intentional study of the Bible is necessary in order to be fully open to the faith to which we are called. As a child I had been exposed to Bible stories and had been involved in church activities. I did not have an intentional study of the Bible until the birth of my son. When Nick was born, I decided that it was necessary for me, as a new father, to understand my role as a parent. I began by reading the Bible from cover to cover. After I had read the Bible, I went back and re-read the Bible in a different translation. I repeated my reading several times. As I traveled to work, I would listen to Bible study on my car radio.

Because I lived in Atlanta, I was in traffic for many hours during the week. That gave me the opportunity to listen to several Bible teachers and to begin to formulate a process for Bible study. I was introduced to the work of William Barclay and his commentary on the New Testament. I purchased the whole set of his books and studied the scripture through Barclay's commentaries. As I indicated, I was also teaching Sunday school and was exposed to Southern Baptist literature regarding various Bible topics. It seemed to me that the more I studied the Bible the more that my understanding increased. I believe that the Holy Spirit allows us to become intellectually engaged to understand and interpret the scripture. My experience has shown me that the Holy Spirit will reveal hidden truths in the scriptures at a particular time when it is necessary for us to have a unique and meaningful understanding of God's word. I have found that at the precise moment when that revelation will have the most impact, an insight into the scriptures is given to me. This is the working of the Holy Spirit. I believe it is a manifestation of the Holy Spirit that leads me in the direction that God would have me to travel.

How then does one come to the ability to trust the Holy Spirit to reveal the truth in the scripture?

We have talked about how we need to use God's gifts in order for us to avail ourselves to the riches that God has in store for us. It seems to me that the more we exercise our faith, use the gifts that God has given us, and rely on the Holy Spirit to lead us, the more ability we gain to trust that God will confront us and lead us to a Damascus Road experience.

I have often thought that one of the reasons that I know that God hears my prayers is because my prayers are answered. When my prayers are answered I am assured that God is listening to me and knows what my needs are and is prepared to respond to them. I think the same is true concerning the work of the Holy Spirit. The more we rely on the Holy Spirit to lead us and to give us a clear understanding of scripture the more faithful we can become in allowing ourselves to trust the Holy Spirit's influence and revelation. Therefore, a combination of diligent study of scripture and a reliance on the Holy Spirit to open our eyes and hearts is necessary.

In Matthew 13, Jesus tells the parable of the sower of seeds. The story tells about how the farmer sowed some of the seeds on the pathway, some of the seeds on rocky ground, and some of the seeds in the briar patch. Some of the seeds fell on good fertile ground. That scripture indicates that Jesus spoke in parables because, some of the audience could not or would not see the truth hidden in that story. Later, His disciples asked Jesus about the meaning of the parable and Jesus stated that He spoke in parables because some are incapable of hearing, even though they hear the sound of someone's voice, or are incapable of seeing even though they have eyes. From that discourse, I think we can say that only those with the requisite amount of faith will be able to understand and act. We have spent some time in recounting how Jesus made a distinction concerning those with little faith and how Hebrews 11 gives us a list of Old Testament heroes that had lots of faith (See Chapter 2 above). It seems to me that by exercising our faith we become more bold in using the faith that we have. If you want to build your muscles lift more and more weight. If you want to build your faith, seek ways to rely on the leadership of the Holy Spirit in your everyday life.

When I was a younger lawyer, I had a case in Rome, Georgia regarding a contractor who was hired to build the state prison near Summerville, Georgia. My client was a devout Christian woman. After we won her case, she and I got into a discussion concerning our reliance on God to deal with our everyday activities. Her position was that God was interested in the minute details of her day-to-day activities. My position, at that time, was that God was only concerned with the larger aspects of our lives and that we had to deal with the small stuff on our own.

I have since come to see the active hand of God in even the small stuff. What caused my change of thought about relying on God's presence in the details of my life? The realization that I have been sealed with the Holy Spirit and Jesus lives within me. Paul said that whatever we do we are to do it as if we were doing it unto God. If God keeps track of all that I do, He must care that I do all things correctly, and thus, He cares about not just the big problems but the small stuff too. How did I come to the understanding that the Holy Spirit dwells within me? It was much like realizing that God answers my prayers. If I rely on the leadership of the Holy Spirit, He will lead me.

As I mentioned earlier, Dr. Stanley (In Touch television broadcast) said that it is the Holy Spirit who tells Christians to refrain from doing things that we should not be doing. Stanley said that as a Christian if you know that something that you are about to do is wrong, that is the Holy Spirit working in your heart to lead you away from trouble. I do not dispute Charles Stanley's assessment of the role of the Holy Spirit in the lives of Christ's followers, but are we not all subject to our own conscience? Even little children know right from wrong to some degree. Christians are still free to disobey the warnings of our conscience at our own peril. On the other hand, if you as a Christian are compelled to move in a new direction it is certainly the leadership of the Holy Spirit opening a new door that you need to go through.

When I become attuned to relying on the leadership of the Holy Spirit, I came to believe that the Holy Spirit will lead me. This may sound like circular reasoning, but it is not. The more we exercise our spiritual nature the more access we have to the Spirit of God and the more willing the Holy Spirit is to do His work in us. While we need to be always on guard that the Holy Spirit is trying to get our attention, there is also the possibility that an evil spirit may be trying to lead us in a completely wrong direction. The actions of Satan and Satan's minions (evil spirits) are the topics of the next chapter.

Chapter 4
The Nature of Evil

Physical, Mental and Spiritual Evil

When I started writing this book, I was thinking about the spiritual inertia that causes us to become stagnate (I used the term couch potatoes probably too many times). We discussed how inertia effects physical objects and how velocity and mass can change an objects direction. We also discussed the emotional toll that can occur when we become stuck in emotional limbo. We remembered how Jonah despite God's calling ran in the wrong direction and had to be swallowed by a big fish and spit out on the beach before he became committed to the Nineveh crusade. We then discussed the spiritual attributes of the heroes of faith found in Hebrews 11. Just like our discussions concerning inertia, the nature of evil has physical, emotional, and spiritual aspects.

Physical Evil

In the gospel of John, the apostle pronounces that Jesus is the light of the world. John contrasts light and darkness contending that light is pure and good while darkness is that by which evil is hidden. John says that Jesus was the light of the world, though the world knew him not. Because the world did not recognize that Jesus was the creator of the world, the world has continued in darkness.

Scientists have discovered that our universe has black holes. These black holes are very powerful and when physical objects come in contact with them, they are crushed. Black holes are so powerful that no light is emitted from them and when light comes near a black hole it is sucked into the unknown reaches of the physical abyss. Additionally, scientists have theorized that all around us is an unknown force referred to as black matter. Today, physicists are devising experiments in order to determine the presence of black matter and to understand its properties. From a physical standpoint the presence of black holes in our universe and the theory that black matter is all around us lends credence to the idea that there is a physical nature to evil.

Mental Evil

When I was still practicing law, I became familiar with the DSM-4. That was the 4th edition of the *Diagnostic and Statistical Manual of Mental Disorders*. The DSM-4 has been replaced by the DSM-5. In that book, there is a listing of all mental and socialization disorders known to mental health care professionals. That reference book is a diagnostic tool that identifies mental health issues so that they can be treated. Among the mental disorders are such issues as alcoholism, depression, schizophrenia, anxiety disorders and many other known psychological issues. Many of these disorders are treated by psychiatrist using the latest pharmacological innovations. Some of the disorders identified in the DSM-5 are treated by psychologist and others are treated by sociologist trained to deal with these mental health issues. While one could state that mental health issues are health issues, mental illness robs those suffering from alcoholism, depression, anxiety disorders and other mental illnesses from functioning in a normal and healthy manner. From this one could say that mental health disorders are a form of evil that exists in the world and that there is an emotional toll to be paid, because of the maleficent nature of these mental disorders.

When Jesus came into this world, He was often called upon to heal individuals with physical, mental, and spiritual health issues. Jesus was called on to cast out demons that caused not only the individual to suffer but also effected the friends and family of the one that was suffering. Do you recall the story of the Gadarenes demoniac in Mark chapter 5? Jesus and His disciples had sailed across the sea of Galilee and came to the area of the Holy Land that is to the northeast of that body of water. When they arrived on the shore, they were confronted by a man who was possessed by a legion of evil spirits. Immediately the possessed man came up to Jesus and demanded to know what the son of God had to do with him.

The demoniac had been living out among the graves and could not be controlled by any of the people around there. They had often tried to bind him with ropes or chains, but he would always escape and would wail and scream and would even cut himself with sharp rocks. Jesus demanded that the evil spirits come out of this poor man and the evil spirits entered into a herd of pigs and drowned themselves in the lake. After Jesus had driven out the evil spirits, the townspeople came and were amazed to find the man in his right mind and with clothes on. The townspeople were frightened by what Jesus had done and demanded that He move on. The man that had been relieved of the evil spirits wanted to become one of Jesus's disciples and travel with Jesus. Instead, Jesus told him to go into the towns around that region and to show the people what changes had come into his life.

Spiritual Evil

Some would say that the mental health issues, that people face today, are not issues of good versus evil. Non-believers do not consider that there are evil spirits that are active in the world today. On the other hand, it seems to me that evil can be found at every turn and that we, as believers, must be constantly on guard not to fall victim to the actions of Satan.

Paul had much to say about the presence of evil in believer's lives. In Ephesians 6:11-12, Paul says "Put on the whole armor of God, that you may be able to withstand the wiles of the devil. For we wrestle not against flesh and blood, but against principalities, against powers, against the rulers of the darkness of the world, against spiritual wickedness in high places." Paul goes on to say that we must equip ourselves with the full armor of spiritual warfare that will allow us to withstand the evil that is around us. (For the most part the spiritual armor that Paul describes is for defensive purposes. Paul does suggest that scripture, the word of God is useful for going on the offense).

I do not know if Paul knew anything about black holes or dark matter, but he certainly knew that there was a spiritual battle going on in the lives of Christians at the time that he wrote his letter to the Ephesians. While we have evidence of the physical properties of dark matter and black holes in the universe and understand the toll that mental illness can exact in the lives of believers and non- believers, the aspect of spiritual warfare sometimes escapes our notice or even worse is ignored even when we become aware that there is a spiritual battle for the hearts and minds of our friends and families.

Is Evil a Part of God's Creation?

A few years ago, in a biography by Walter Isaacson entitled *Jobs*, concerning the life of Steve Jobs, one of the founders of Apple Computer, it is related that Mr. Jobs turned his back on Christianity because he could not understand why there is evil in the world if God exist. Jobs' reasoning was that if God exists, He is good and is incapable of creating evil. Because evil is in the world, and we all recognize that there is evil and there are people consumed by evil, there must not be a Christian God. On the other hand, the apostle Peter tells us that God exist, and that God is personified in Jesus Christ, who Paul met one day on the road to Damascus. At the same time, evil in the form of a devil also known as Satan, is in the world and is seeking whom he may devour. In 1 Peter 5:8, Peter writes, "Be sober, be vigilant; because your adversary the devil walks about like a roaring lion, seeking whom he may devour."

So, we have a dilemma, God created the universe including black holes and dark matter. On the other hand, God is good. (That was the first Bible verse that I learned as a child Luke18;19). As I stated before, John in the 4th gospel in the New Testament, tells us that Jesus is the light of the world and in Him there is no darkness at all. The Bible is full of comparisons in which good is depicted as light and evil is depicted as darkness. The contrast between light and dark shows us that in order to understand the difference between good and evil we must be able to understand the nature of light as well as the nature of darkness. From a scientific standpoint, without light we would not be able to differentiate objects that might be placed in front of us.

Once, I traveled to Mammoth Cave just outside of Bowling Green, Kentucky. I took a tour of the cave and at one point our guide had all the lights turned off at a place where no light could be seen. We were in complete darkness, and I could not see anything. It was very strange, I heard the sound of water dripping from the roof of the cave, but I could not determine where the drops might fall. However, as soon as the lights came back on everything became clear. There were beautiful rock formations all around, there were other people in the tour group that I was in, and I could see the path that I needed to take in order to get out of that cave (I am not claustrophobic, but just the same I did not want to stay in the cave more than just visiting).

Had I stayed in the cave without any light I may have wandered around in there and may still be wandering without knowing how to escape. By contrast as soon as the lights came on the pathway out of the cave became clear. Similarly, without Jesus I am in spiritual darkness, and I do not know which way to turn or to differentiate between right and wrong. When Jesus entered into my life, and I fully give my life to Him, He led me out of darkness and into a life that is full of light.

What then can we say? Did God create darkness so that we could understand the necessity of light in our spirit? Is there a form of spiritual darkness that can only be overcome when we come to know the Light of the World? I have tried to reason this spiritual dilemma in my own consciousness. I believe that it is almost impossible to know that there is a need for light unless there is also darkness. However, did God create evil just so that we would know that God is good?

Consider Job, not Steve Jobs, but the Job in book of Job in the Old Testament. The book of Job is perhaps the oldest book in the Bible. In it we find a conversation between God and Satan. God relates that Job is a really good man. Satan tells God that Job is good because God has blessed him with good friends, a good family, and plenty of wealth. The Bible relates that it is true Job has a good thing going. Job is one of the wealthiest men in town, lives in a nice house, has a bunch of good kids and that they are well behaved. In fact, early in the story, Job's children are having a big celebration at one of the Job's son's houses.

The devil tells God that Job would not be so good if all his family, friends, and possessions were taken away from him. God gives Satan permission to afflict Job in order to prove Job's goodness. All of a sudden, Job loses all his wealth, a storm comes up and all of its children are killed, and Job has nothing left. Even with these losses, Job still finds favor with God because he remains true to God and continues to worship God. To up the ante, Satan tells God that Job would not be so good if he personally were to suffer. Again, God gives Satan permission to afflict Job's health. Satan causes sores to appear all over Job's body. Job is made to physically suffer and to add insult to injury Mrs. Job tells him that he ought to curse God and die.

Next, four of Job's friends show up while Job is suffering and in the guise of offering comfort and understanding to Job, each one of them begin to question Job as to the cause of his suffering. Job's friends seemed to agree that Job must have done some great sinful act in order for God's wrath to have put Job into such a bad place. Each of Job's so called, friends stand around and debate with Job about what is the cause of Job's suffering and the evil that has befallen him. Of course, neither of these guys nor Job nor even Mrs. Job, have been privy to the conversations that went on in heaven between God and Satan. All that this group of individuals can see is the suffering that Job is forced to endure and based on their own experience must blame Job's bad condition on someone or something that Job has done.

Before long, Job begins to ask himself, "Why is it that God has caused the affliction that I am suffering?" Finally, Job demands that God answer his questions concerning what has gone wrong in his life, and much to Job's surprise, God makes himself available to answer Job's question. However, I am not sure that our old friend Job got the answer for which he was looking. God comes to Job in the form of a whirlwind. Job wants to know how is it that God has caused the calamity in Job's life and why did it happen; because Job thought that he was doing everything right. We often ask the same questions. That is, why am I suffering and what have I done to cause this to happen to me? In Job's case, this all came about because Satan challenged God concerning Job's faithfulness and goodness.

When God spoke to Job, He responds to Job's questions with God's own questions. God seems to want Job to understand that Job does not have the same perspective as God. God asks Job, "Were you there when I created the earth, when I put the stars in the sky, when I created the oceans and put all living creatures in the ocean and on the earth? And by the way Job, are you able to understand what has gone on in heaven? Do you know about the great sea monsters and even the herds of elephants that roam the earth? In today's language the questions would be more like, do you understand exactly how I created the universe, or are you just guessing?"

What are we to take from this ancient lesson from the book of Job? Do we really believe that Satan confronts God in order to test someone like me? Should I hold God responsible when bad things happen to good people? By the way where did Satan come from anyway? These same questions have been asked since ancient times and we do not know fully how to answer such questions. We seem only to be able to answer the questions with more questions.

Again, I can only speculate but if you allow me to speculate, here is what I think. I believe that Satan is an active force in the world. I believe that Satan tries to disrupt our relationships with God and makes us question whether God is active in our lives and whether Jesus really loves us. Self-doubt is Satan's most used and effective tool in tormenting people today. I do not know how Satan came into being or why he is able to battle with the goodness of God in our lives. I do not know if God allows Satan to torment us or if our suffering is a test by God to see if we are truly committed to Him, but I do know that bad things can happen to really good people, and it is the measure of a good person's commitment to God that makes all the difference in their lives.

I went to law school in New Orleans and joined the Saint Charles Ave. Baptist Church while I lived in the Garden District of New Orleans. The pastor of the church was Avery Lee. His wife attended the church when I first started going there. Her name was Anne. When I first met Anne Lee, her face was bandaged, and she seemed to be in pain. After a while I learned that Anne had cancer and it was eating away at the bones in her face. At first, it was very difficult for me to even look at her. After I got to know her a little bit better, I realized what a saintly person she was. She never complained, despite losing eyesight, she was always helpful to whoever needed her help. Anne continued to suffer with cancer, and it eventually spread to her brain, and she was no longer able to function, but even so she lived out her days with a grace and confidence that God would take care of her and her family. I learned to overlook the suffering and the ugliness that the cancer was causing and see her as a loving, kind, generous Christian who lived out her faith to the end. I can only hope to live such an inspirational life. The physical evil of the cancer was not able to overcome the spiritual beauty of Ann Lee's faith in Jesus.

Jesus's Life and the Presence of Evil

The first four books of the New Testament of the Bible, give us a picture of the life of Jesus especially from the time that He started His ministry in Galilee until the time of His crucifixion and resurrection. My reading of The Gospels leads me to believe that Jesus was well aware of the presence of evil throughout His ministry.

Shortly after Jesus was baptized in the river Jordan by John the Baptist, Jesus went into the desert and fasted for 40 days. While He was fasting, He was tempted by Satan and had to overcome these temptations in order to establish the parameters of His ministry. Satan physically tempted Jesus to turn stones into bread. Jesus responded, "Man shall not live on bread alone but on every word that comes from the mouth of God." Satan then tempted Jesus from an emotional standpoint by saying to Jesus even if you throw yourself off a tall building the angels will come and rescue you as a proof that you are who you say you are. Lastly, Satan tempted Jesus spiritually by telling Jesus that if Jesus would fall down and worship Satan that Satan would deliver the world to Jesus. Jesus responded, "Away from me, Satan! For it is written: 'Worship the Lord your God and serve Him only'." (Matthew 4:1-11)

Jesus then began His ministry in Galilee and, leaders of the Jewish church almost immediately started to question Jesus's authority. At first these Pharisees merely ask questions concerning whether Jesus was following the law or what Jesus's interpretation of the law might be.

As time went on, Jesus's ministry started to grow and His popularity among the people increased. Of course, that would have happened because of the way that Jesus was healing all those who are afflicted by disease, blindness, and demon possession. Additionally, almost everyone except the religious leader's recognized the authority apparent in His preaching and teaching. The Jewish leaders became more concerned about the impact Jesus was having on the people. There came times when the Jewish leaders confronted Jesus and tried to trick Jesus into making mistakes in His theology. The Jewish leaders would do such things as bring a woman who was caught in adultery before Jesus and make Jesus declare whether He would follow the law and have the woman stoned to death.

In each of these situations, Jesus would reply to their efforts to trap Jesus, by changing the focus of the discussion and turning the question back on the Pharisees. Jesus asked the Pharisees who brought the woman, whom the Pharisees claimed to have caught in the very act of adultery, to Him, if they were without sin, and if they were without sin, if they could cast the first stone. Guess what, one by one the Pharisees dropped their stones and moved away. Jesus looked at the woman and asked where have your accusers gone. I think she said, "I don't know," to which Jesus said, "I do not accuse you either, but go and sin no more."

Jesus was not condoning adultery but was not willing to kill the woman just because of the evil motives of the Pharisees, either. Jesus taught that we should not judge, lest we be judged by the same judgment by which we judge others. The evil in the hearts of the Pharisees, and their willingness to be judgmental, was by far of more concern to Jesus than the fact that they had brought an adulteress before The Prince of Peace. (John 7:53- 8:11) As Jesus's popularity with the people increased, the more hate filled the hearts of the Jewish leaders.

Jesus was both human and the divine Son of God and He had been with God from the beginning. The Bible reminds us that before creation that the world was without form and void and darkness was on the face of the earth. The story does not start there however, because "In the beginning God created..." God created the light and separated the light from the darkness. Remember John's gospel? In the prologue, John who was with Jesus during His earthly ministry, announces that "In the beginning was the Word, and the Word was with God. The same was in the beginning with God. All things were made by Him; and without Him was not anything made that was made. And the Word was made flesh and dwelt among us." (John 1:1-17) The Word was also the Light of the world so that all could see the nature and likeness of God. I have heard it said that John's prologue takes us back before the creation of the heaven and the earth to the point where the Creator is in existence, but His creation activity has not started. Jesus states that He is the light of the world. John 8:12.

Eventually, Jesus announced to His disciples that He was going to go to Jerusalem and there He would be arrested, abused by the authorities, killed and He would arise from the dead after three days. The Bible indicates that His disciples really did not understand what Jesus was talking about. However, it is clear, that Jesus knew exactly what was going to happen and He knew what was eventually going to get Him killed. It was the hatred in the hearts of those who would not believe that Jesus was the chosen one of God.

In the Old Testament, Isaiah prophesizes that the one who would be the Lamb of God, would have to suffer. Isaiah told us that with His stripes we would be healed. (Isaiah 53:5) In other places in the Old Testament there are many references to the suffering servant and how the Messiah would be revealed. Even though the Pharisees and the religious leaders of Jesus day knew the prophecies there was a failure to recognize that Jesus fulfilled all the prophecies concerning the suffering servant.

What could have created the hatred in these religious men that would be so extreme as to cause them to not only want Jesus dead but to do it in such a brutal manner? Again, consider our old friend Paul. Paul was a contemporary of Jesus and prior to the day Paul was going to Damascus, Paul also hated Jesus and those that followed Jesus. Had Satan entered into the hearts and minds of the Jews that persecuted and killed Jesus? They certainly were not very tolerant of any threat to their religious beliefs.

They thought that they had a corner on what was right and that they should and could impose their beliefs on anyone that was not subject to their control.

Jesus was tacitly a threat to them even though Jesus had told His disciples and those that listened to His teachings that He was not there to overthrow or change the religious practices of the Pharisees or the other religious leaders. Jesus's intent was to show the very nature and grace of God. The Pharisees and the religious leaders were not so much interested in the nature and presents of God as they were in keeping their authority in place.

Fyodor Dostoevsky, in *Brothers Karamazov*, tells the very interesting story set in the days of the Spanish Inquisition in the city of Seville, Spain. In that story, Jesus encounters a funeral procession and stops to raise a mother's only son from the dead. In that book the author tells us that immediately Jesus is arrested and there is a colloquy between Jesus and the local cardinal of the Catholic Church. The conversation, between the cardinal and Jesus is fairly one sided. The cardinal tells Jesus that Jesus is interfering with what has become the right and authority of the church. The cardinal knows that he is speaking to Jesus but tells Jesus that the church now has the authority to keep the people in line and to assert the standards that keep the church prosperous. The cardinal tells Jesus that the people really need the church to set the standards that the church needs to set. The church can tell the people what they must do in order to have their sins forgiven and to pay homage to the authority of the religious leaders. Jesus is about to upset the applecart by coming and showing compassion to this poor woman and her child without first seeking permission from the church. The church will not tolerate Jesus's interference in the churches' authority. For that offense Jesus is going to have to pay the ultimate price again and be burned at the stake.

Dostoevsky of course was writing fiction, but his insight into those who assert authority in the name of God share a common pattern of behavior. In the hearts of those who are in authority, or are claiming to be in authority, but who are not submitting to the authority of God, are submitting themselves to the authority of Satan. Consider Jesus message to the church at Smyrna in the book of Revelations where He says that the pseudo-Jews are really the Synagogue of Satan. (Revelations 2: 8-11)

Remember that in the beginning there was God but at the same time darkness and a formless void existed. It was only when God created light and separated the light from darkness that mankind was able to comprehend that there is a way out of darkness. When Jesus arrived, there was still a darkness in the hearts of men that caused mankind to be separated from God. Jesus came to provide a light in the hearts of men that would allow them to comprehend the presence of God and understand that mankind had been under the control of Satan since created man was removed from the garden of Eden. God allowed mankind to be on its own and make its own choices concerning whether to follow God or to give in to the sinful nature that mankind inherited from the start.

I think about my own children, when they were still toddlers and just learning to communicate with me and their mother, they were prone to tell lies. I would ask, "Nick, did you just hit your sister." Nick would reply, "no." "But Nick, I just saw you hit your sister." Again, Nick would reply "no it wasn't me." I am sure we have all experienced similar discussions with our children. It is not so much that these conversations are not unusual, but it is the fact that our children from the very start of their lives are prone to tell lies. Is it part of our human nature that we are sinners from the very start? Therefore, can it not also be said that the darkness that was throughout the universe indicated that without the light that God spoke into existence, that the whole universe was evil. Without light the universe would be just like when I was in Mammoth Cave and the tour guide turned out the lights. But when Jesus arrived it was as if the tour guide turned on the lights and a pathway to God became clear. Not only that, Jesus, showed us that the light can triumph over the darkness. Jesus's resurrection from the dead was like a bright light went on in heaven that illuminated the path out of spiritual darkness and gave Christians a pathway home.

While the pathway to God became clear when Jesus arose from the dead, there are still many obstacles that prevent people from taking advantage of the light. Satan is still very active, and many people are not interested in coming to the light because they enjoy darkness.

Existentialism

One way that this generation shows its interest in not seeking a pathway to God, is that they look inwardly and do not recognize the existence of the authority of God. In the 100 Psalm, we are reminded that, "Know ye that the Lord He is God. It is He that hath made us, and not we ourselves; we are His people, and the sheep of his pasture." In contrast to the idea is that there is a God, is a focus on our own importance.

The most influential philosophy today, is that of Existentialism. Existentialism is defined as "A philosophical theory or approach which emphasizes the existence of the individual person as a free and responsible agent determining their own development through acts of the will." Wikipedia states that existentialism it is a form of philosophical inquiry that explores the problem of human existence and centers on the lived experience of the thinking, feeling, acting individual.

Too often, men seek to create God in man's own image. There is a complete failure on the part of mankind to recognize that God created and that I am a part, and only a part, of God's creation. Especially in a country like the United States, where there is a great deal of freedom, the individualism established at the start of this country has made the individual the primary focus of life. We admire the self-made man. We envy the athlete that can put the team on his shoulders and carry the entire burden of the victory. We revel in stories in which the individual overcomes great odds in order to defeat those that would seek to destroy them. There are very few of us who do not enjoy movies, and books in which the hero has been abused by the villain and then by sheer strength of will is able to overcome and put the bad guy in his place. I think that that is probably the most common plot in movies and books available for consumption.

There are many who even equate the story of Jesus to such a plot. They see in Jesus someone who is tormented by His accusers but despite the hatred in the Pharisees' hearts, Jesus overcomes and puts the Pharisees in their place. That, however, is not exactly what happened. Jesus obeyed the will of God and went to the cross in obedience to God's requirement that Jesus pay the price for my sins. Jesus did not seek to fulfill His own will but submitted Himself to the will of God. In the garden of Gethsemane Jesus prayed that if it was in God's will that He would not like to have to suffer the agony and torment to which He was going to be put. Jesus prayed, "Not my will but thy will be done." (Matthew 26:42)

How many of us are willing to give up our own resolve in order to stay consistent with the path that the Holy Spirit has set for us? The existential man would have no problem in saying to himself, "Well, is this good for me and what am I going to get out of this?" The life of the existential man is consistent with capitalism and even Calvinism. By that I mean that the existential man seeks to gain from whatever in which he is engaged. Calvinism puts an emphasis on a man's individual productivity as a measure of his worthiness and in turn as a sign of God's favor. That summery of Calvinism is not intended to summarize the tenants of John Calvin's beliefs but only to consider the extent to which his beliefs have been used to distort the words of Jesus concerning the relationship between God and mankind. If Jesus would have put the emphasis on His own wellbeing, He would not have stepped down from heaven, taken on the form of a servant, and submitted Himself to the cross. (Philippians 2: 5-11)

How then do we recognize the inconsistency of the Christian life with that of the existential man? We as a human species have struggled with this dilemma since the beginning. Remember the story of Cain and Abel. Able was a godly man and wanted to please God by doing as God had commanded. Cain, on the other hand, was more interested in doing what Cain wanted to do. That eventually led to animosity between these two brothers and Cain killed Able. Able recognized the authority of God. Abel recognized that Able was not in charge of Abel's life but was willing to put God first. Cain on the other hand, wanted to put Cain first.

After the children of Israel left bondage in Egypt and appeared before God at the foot of Mount Sinai, God provided to Moses the Ten Commandments. (Exodus 20) There God told the people of Israel, "I am the Lord your God, I have brought you out of the land of Egypt, out of the house of bondage. You shall have no other gods before me." With that Commandment, God establishes His supremacy as the force in our lives to which we will be held accountable.

So, we must decide whether we are accountable to God or only accountable to our own selves. In other words, we must decide if we are our own God; or do we see God as being "Our Father in heaven." If we are only accountable to ourselves, and an existential man, then we are like Cain and when asked, "Where is your brother?," can glibly reply "Am I my brother's keeper?"

How can we recognize when we have placed other gods before the one true God? I think the real question is "Are we diligently seeking to know God by asking The Holy Spirit to guide our hearts and minds to understand God's will in our lives?" When Jesus provided the model prayer to His disciples (Matthew 6: 9-13) He said to pray as follows: "Thy will be done in earth, as it is in heaven." If Jesus is asking us to pray that God's will shall be accomplished in our lives just as if God was telling His angels to do this and that, then when God answers our prayers, we know exactly who is in charge of our lives. I know that I have said it before in this book, we know we are heading in the right direction and that God hears us when we have answered prayers. I think it is vitally important in our lives that we pray and have an expectation, that our prayers will be answered. When we pray with the expectation that our prayers will be answered we know that we have a Father in heaven and that we are not so self-reliant as to exclude God from our lives.

But when we act as if God does not exist and that we are completely in charge over our own lives we become existentialist. Being an existentialist robs us of faith, causes us to turn inwardly and to judge others by the criteria that we ourselves have created. We are free then to be controlled by our materialistic instincts and are free to take advantage of even those who love us. Is that not exactly what happened to Cain? I don't know exactly what the relationship between Cain and Abel was, but I would suspect that they acted just like brothers. Perhaps they played practical jokes on each other, or one rooted for one football team and the other rooted for its rival. They probably got along OK. However, Able was a godly man and believed that God was in control of his life, and he wanted to please God. Cain, not so much. I believe Cain was probably the first existentialist, because he only acted in his self- interest.

We live in the ultimate materialistic society. Statistical evidence has shown that belief in God is on the decline in the United States. Europe has long ago turned from a belief in God to become a materialistic society. It seems that only in countries like South Korea and to some extent China, that Christianity is on the rise. There is obviously a very good reason that the 1st of the Ten Commandments requires a steadfast acknowledgement and belief that there is only one God and that we can have no other gods before Him.

As I am writing this book, there is a dramatic increase in mass shootings throughout the United States. In recent days it has been reported that there have been over 250 mass homicides in the USA within the first six months of 2021. The shootings have been in every part of the country. Some of the homicides have taken place in grocery stores, at Walmart, in massage parlors, random shootings on the street, and even in churches. News reports have indicated that those carrying out these mass shootings are often troubled individuals who on many occasions take their own lives as a part of the mass shooting. While we are certainly speculating as to the mental stability of the individual shooters, I think it is safe to say that none of these individuals are godly.

We can safely say that godly people do not commit mass homicides. I think that those committing these horrific crimes are only concerned about their own self and certainly not about the impact that they are going to have on the lives of their victims and the family members of their victims. If they believed in God (discounting for the moment those who are delusional) they would not have acted in the manner that would cause them to go out and gun down innocent people in the streets.

Is it possible then, that Paul's warning in Ephesians 6, that there is a spiritual battle going on all around us is more likely than not? Spiritual warfare, truly represents the current state of affairs throughout the world? If that is the case, and it surely is, then we as Christians must take all necessary steps to combat the evil that is in the world. We combat evil by becoming godly.

Jesus expressed godliness in His Sermon on the Mount, when He said, "Blessed are the poor in spirit, for theirs is the Kingdom of heaven." (Matthew 5: 3) When a person is "poor in spirit", that person recognizes that he is not alone and that his spirit must submit itself to the Holy Spirit. When the Holy Spirit reigns within our life we are under the control of our heavenly Father, and we allow the spirit to put God first.

Paul said we combat evil by putting on the whole armor of God. That would include the breastplate of righteousness and all the other attributes of spiritual armor that is necessary to stand as a faithful follower of God and to withstand the devil. A person that puts God at the forefront of his life is keeping the all-important First Commandment. Jesus taught His followers (including us) that the Kingdom of God is at hand. The Kingdom of God is at hand because our Lord and Savior Jesus Christ dwells in us. When Jesus dwells in us we become godly and come to understand that we are only passing through this world and are on our way to the Kingdom of heaven. Temptations and evil can be over-come, and we can become perfect even as our Father in heaven is perfect. (Matthew 5: 48)

Chapter 5
Living A Perfect Life

Is it possible to live a perfect life? Are we to take the words of Jesus in Matthew 5: 48 literally, or is there some other meaning to Jesus's admonition to live perfectly? I have heard Matthew 5: 48 interpreted in a way in which it seems as if the word "perfect" should be interpreted to mean to live a mature Christian life. (I understand the debate concerning whether the Bible should be taken literally or is subject to interpretation. Because I can neither translate the original Greek nor Hebrew nor any other language that the writers of the Bible used, I rely on the scholars who translated the Bible into English and on the Holy Spirit for my understanding of scripture.) On the other hand, Jesus said that we are to live perfectly as our Father in heaven is perfect.

If we believe that Jesus equated the way we are to live with the very nature of God, then we must determine for ourselves whether God is perfect and are we capable of living a godly life. I believe that God is perfect, and that God created the heavens and the earth and saw that it was perfect. God created man, and saw that men and women are created in the image of God and are therefore perfectly created and as a Christian I am capable of living a life that is perfect. What then can keep Christians from living a perfect life? See 1 John 5:18 where John the close friend of Jesus states as follows: "We know that anyone born of God does not continue to sin; the One who was born of God keeps them safe, and the evil one cannot harm them. We know that we are the children of God and that the whole world is under the control of the evil one. We know also that the son of God has come and has given us understanding, so that we may know Him who is true. And we are in

Him who is true by being in His son Jesus Christ. He is the true God and eternal life."

The apostle John also wrote at 1 John 1:8-10 that states: "If we say that we have no sin, we deceive ourselves, and the truth is not in us. If we confess our sins, He is faithful and just to forgive our sins, and to cleanse us from all unrighteousness. If we say that we have not sinned, we make Him a liar, and His word is not in us." Therefore, John acknowledged that as Christians we have sin in our lives. Because God cannot accept sinners into His kingdom, we need something or someone to cover for us so that God will accept us even though our human nature causes us to sin.

John, the apostle, was a close friend of Jesus. According to the gospels, John with the other disciples had an approximately 3 years fellowship with Jesus. During that time, John became well acquainted with Jesus's teachings and His relationship with God. John was there when Jesus gave His Sermon on the Mount. John was there when Jesus healed thousands of sick and dying people and exorcised people possessed with demons. John saw the feeding of the 5000 and watched Jesus walk across the top of lake Galilee. John sat next to Jesus at the Last Supper. John was there when they crucified my Lord. John out-ran Peter to the open tomb on Easter Sunday and was in the upper room when Jesus appeared after His resurrection.

You could say in all honesty, that John the Apostle had an intimate and close relationship with Jesus Christ. That relationship allowed John to form an accurate opinion regarding the characteristics of a Christian's fellowship with Jesus. I believe that what John is telling us in his writing at 1 John 1:8-

10 and 1 John 5:18, is that because we have a human nature that we have not totally discarded, we remain prone to temptation and sin. However, when we accept Jesus into our lives and submit ourselves to the leadership of the Holy Spirit, we take on more of the attributes of God and thus become godlier.

In the 5th chapter of 1 John, we are told that, "We know that whosoever is born of God does not sin; but he that is begotten of God keeps himself sinless, and that the wicked one does not touch him. And we know that we are of God and the whole world is full of wickedness. And we know that the Son of God has come into the world and has given us an understanding that we may know the true Son of God, and we are in the Holy Spirit, and He is true, even as His son Jesus Christ. Jesus is the true God, and in Him is eternal life." (My paraphrase)

I think what John is trying to tell us is that Jesus expects us to be perfect. God created mankind in the image of God. God put His attributes into us. God then provided to us Jesus with whom we should pattern our lives. When we ask Jesus into our lives, He provides us with the Holy Spirit. The Holy Spirit convicts us of our sins and leads us in the ways of righteousness. By His death on the cross, He has offered Himself as a living sacrifice for my and our sins. Once I have accepted Jesus into my life my sins are forgiven and are covered by His blood. We can trust the Holy Spirit to show us how to escape temptation if we listen to the Holy Spirit's guidance. On the other hand, when we mess up (and all of us will mess up) He will forgive us and set us on the right path.

In *Pilgrim's Progress*, John Bunyan shows us that even Christian (the main character of Bunyan's allegory) fell into the slough of despond. There are many who fall into the slough of despond and many who cannot escape. It is only when Christian earnestly calls on God to lift him out of the muck and the mire of temptation that the Angel comes and sets Christian back on the pathway to the celestial city. Is it not that life is just like that? Christians are capable of living a perfect life and staying on the pathway to heaven. When temptations, and the cares of the world, and the allure of money throw us out of our Christian walk, it is only the love of Jesus that sets us back on the right road. We can stay focused and can be perfect even as our Father in heaven is perfect because He has made us in His image with the expectation of perfection.

Chapter 6
The Necessity of Christian Fellowship

Have you ever tried to live as a hermit? Are you antisocial? If you are a hermit or antisocial, you are not a normal person. As we all know, we humans desire the society of others and understand that God has put into us a need to have fellowship with other human beings. Psychologists tell us that normal humans desire to be with other normal humans. Perhaps the most human desire is to form a relationship with another human and to seek the comfort and love of a partner. Most often our partner is either a husband or wife. The Bible tells us that it is normal for a man to marry a wife and that the two shall become as one. We engage in elaborate marriage ceremonies and often spend enormous amounts of money to stage our wedding vows.

We humans also enjoy the fellowship of our friends and family. We want to be connected to others with whom we are familiar. On occasions we even engage in the ritual of college football in which we make ourselves look like a herd of fans and engage in the ritual of wearing team colors and screaming for our humans to beat up on the other humans that are not part of our fan loyalty. We engage in these rituals because for thousands of years we have adapted a tribal mentality when living in groups. A tribal mentality means that we separate ourselves into a group and look at others with a "us versus them" point of view.

While I am not a psychiatrist or psychologist, I do recognize that humans like to group themselves into various tribes to the exclusion of others.

We separate ourselves by race, gender, nationality, sports team affiliation, brand of cars we like, geographical region, and all sorts of other preferences that we have. In E. O. Wilson's, *The Meaning of Human Existence*, the author, and ardent University of Alabama football fan, tells us that we all like to be a part of a tribe and exclude those who are not in our tribe. We want to associate with like- minded people. From early childhood we learn that we are a part of a group and that our group has unique qualities that sets members of the group apart from those that are not a part of our tribe. Animals especially mammals, also group themselves by their species and group.

When our group is threatened by an outside force or other group, we tend to close ranks and protect the integrity of our group. When our group succeeds in its endeavor (our college team beats the living daylights out of our rival) we are overwhelmed with joy and celebrate our victory, even though we may not have fully participated in the contest. We revel in the exploits of our group. We are prone to become nationalistic in our love of country. We are likely to say, "I will support my country whether it's right or wrong." In a family setting we are likely to take up for our brothers or other siblings no matter what they have done. We are prone to defend the brand that we choose even if there is something better, just because our group favors one brand over another. Political parties are based on the group's decision to support one candidate over another even if that candidate says that he could get away with murder by shooting someone on 5th Ave.

Is it healthy or even the right thing to do to support our group at the expense of those who are outside of our tribe? Does supporting the group keep us from learning to appreciate the diversity of the population around us? There has been hatred of certain minority racial groups in the United States since colonial days. Anti-Semitism has plagued the Jewish population of the world since history has been recorded. In recent days, there has been an outbreak of violence against people of Asian background in the United States. A civil war was fought in the United States because the general population (both in the South and in the North) did not believe that blacks were created equally to whites. Hatred has filled the hearts of men and women because of the differences between racial groups, and it is just because they are different from us.

I believe someday we will all have to answer for how we have treated others even if they are outside of our group. In the 25th chapter of Matthew, Jesus tells us that there will be a judgment before the great white throne in heaven. The sheep and the goats will be separated. To the group identified as sheep, the Lord will say, "Well done good and faithful servants. because when I was hungry you gave me something to eat, when I was thirsty you gave me something to drink, when I was a stranger, you took me in, when I was naked you clothed me, when I was sick you came to comfort me, and when I was in jail you visited me." Those to whom the Lord was speaking replied, "When did we see you when you were hungry, thirsty, naked, a stranger, sick or in jail." Lord will say when you did it to the least of these you did it to Me, therefore go into your reward.

Jesus will say to the other group (designated as goats), depart from me you that are guilty, because you will wind up in the place of torment that is prepared by the devil and his angels. Because "When I was a stranger, you did not take me in, when I was naked, you let me stay un-clothed, when I was sick and in prison you failed to visit me." These that the Lord cursed said, "When did we see you hungry, thirsty, naked, a stranger in our midst, sick and in prison." Jesus will reply when you failed to take care of the least of these among you.

What is Jesus trying to tell us by relating the story of the sheep and the goats? I think a little deeper inquiry must be made. Remember, Jesus had sent his disciples to the towns and villages in order to minister to a larger segment of the population. (Matthew 10: 1-32) Also, just as Jesus was ascending into heaven (Matthew 28: 18-20), Jesus told His followers that they should go into the world and teach everyone to observe all the instructions that Jesus had given. His followers were to then baptize everyone in the name of the Father, the Son and the Holy Spirit. Jesus said that as you go to do this, that Jesus would be with these witnesses always even into the end of the world.

During the early part of His ministry, Jesus was confronted by a lawyer who asked Jesus, "What shall I do to inherit eternal life?" Jesus asked the lawyer, "because you are a lawyer what is your reading of the law?" The lawyer replied, "Love the Lord your God with all your heart, soul and strength, and with all your mind: and love your neighbor as yourself." The lawyer wanted to justify himself, so he continued to question Jesus and asked, "Who is my neighbor?" (Luke 10: 25- 37).

Jesus, in reply to the lawyer, told the story of "the Good Samaritan." In that story, a man was going down to Jericho from Jerusalem. On the way he was confronted by a gang of thieves who beat the man, stripped him of his clothes, and stole his money. The injured man was left by the side of the road naked, bleeding and unable to get up because he was half dead.

After a while, a priest came by but when he saw this man who had been robbed, he crossed to the other lane and went around. Likewise, a Levite, a person that performed religious functions at the synagogue, came by, saw the poor man who had been beaten, but also passed by on the other side of the street. Lastly, a Samaritan, a man from the wrong side of the tracks, came by, saw the beaten man, had pity on him, dressed his wounds, put him on his animal, took him down to the nearest hotel, ministered to him, and when he was about to leave, told the innkeeper that if the poor man who had been beaten, stripped of his clothes, and robbed, needed anything more than what had already been provided, that this Samaritan would pay it when he returned.

Jesus then asked the lawyer, "Which of the three that came by the robbed man acted as his neighbor?" The lawyer who could not make himself say the Samaritan (probably because of the group hatred between Jews and Samaritans) replied, "The one who showed mercy." Jesus said go and do likewise.

You may ask, what does all this have to do with the topic of fellowship? I'm glad you asked. I believe what Jesus is telling us, is that "A friend in need is a friend indeed." It seems that Jesus is making a big point out of how we respond to the needs of others. Jesus is concerned with how we respond to the needs of all those around us, whether those that are in need live next door or are strangers. Jesus seems to go out of his way to tell us that it does not matter whether the person in need is even someone we know or even someone you can recognize as being from your tribe. The person that is in need, may even be somebody that we do not particularly care to be around. We still must respond to the needs of others wherever we may find them, and whatever their need may be.

Obviously, the man ministered to by the Good Samaritan, had need of physical care. Jesus did not stop at that point because when He ascended into heaven, He told his followers to also meet the spiritual needs of those that they encountered all over the world, as well. I believe that Jesus's definition of fellowship requires that we actively seek to encounter people in all walks of life for the purpose of introducing Jesus to them. I take Jesus's Commandment that we go into the world to teach and baptize seriously. If that makes me an evangelical, then that is exactly what I am. I believe it was for that purpose that Jesus confronted Paul on the Damascus Road. I believe it was for that reason that John the Apostle and the other writers of the gospels have laid out these events so that we can see how Jesus requires us to act as long as we are on this earth.

In other words, Christianity is not really a religion, but it is an active submission to the instructions and commandments of Jesus to meet the needs of people. When the lawyer asked Jesus, "What must I do to inherit the eternal life?" The response was not to join the First Baptist Church, it was not to give to the building fund, it was not to be in awe of a good preacher or teacher, and it certainly was not to join an exclusive club that looks down their noses at those that are less fortunate. What Jesus said was love God completely and love your neighbor as yourself. That means, we are to understand the physical, mental, and spiritual needs of those that we encounter, while we are still in this world, and do our very best to meet those needs.

Christians have been doing that very thing since Jesus sent His disciples into the surrounding communities to minister to people's needs. (Luke 10: 1-16) His disciples were told not to take with them extra shoes or a bag of money, but His disciples were to meet people, stay in their houses, eat their food, heal the sick, cast out demons and do whatever was necessary in order to minister to the needs of those that they encountered. The disciples were to tell the people that welcomed the disciples, that the Kingdom of God was at hand. Interestingly, Jesus told His disciples that if people rejected the disciples, and questioned their authority, to leave that town and go on to another place and shake even the dust off their sandals in the town that rejected the disciples. That would be a sign to the community that by their rejection of God's favor they would have no place in God's Kingdom. It would be better for those that were in wicked Sodom than those that rejected the disciples. When you think of what was happening; by rejecting the disciples and their ministry, the people were actually rejecting Jesus, and by rejecting Jesus they were rejecting God who sent Jesus.

We as Christians need to have fellowship as we go throughout our neighborhoods, our cities, our states and to the uttermost parts of the world. It seems to me that Jesus is telling us that we must have fellowship with every living being that we encounter. Christians are therefore not to exclude others merely because of their differences with us. Christians are to embrace not only fellow Christians, but also sinners and non-Christians in the hope that they will become Christians. The non- exclusiveness of Christianity is indeed a unique quality of those who follow Jesus.

While I say that Christianity is non-exclusive, in reality even we Christians have a history of exclusion. Currently, I am attending a Southern Baptist church in Glen, Mississippi. I am still a member of the Peachtree Baptist Church in Atlanta but have been away from that church for the last two years. Several years ago, Peachtree Baptist was also a member of the Southern Baptist convention and a member of the Georgia Baptist convention. As a congregation we withdrew from those organizations because of the Southern Baptist teachings regarding the place of women in the church. Peachtree Baptist became associated with the Co-operative Baptist Fellowship that I often refer to as the Jimmy Carter Baptist. (President Jimmy Carter was one of the founders of the Co-operative Baptist Fellowship).

The reason for the withdrawal was that Southern Baptist sought to exclude any of its member churches that allowed women to hold the position of pastor in the church or even to be ordained as deacons. Peachtree Baptist had had women deacons for many years and felt as if they should not be told that they could not call a female pastor. In a sense, the Southern Baptists excluded those who did not believe as they did regarding the place of women in the church. I still have many friends and family members who belong to Southern Baptist Churches; I still respect those that attend the Southern Baptist churches and seek to have fellowship with them whenever I can. On the other hand, I do not believe as they do regarding the place of women in the church. Over the years I have been friends with and have fellowshipped with many Jewish friends. I have been invited to Jewish weddings, funerals, bat and bar mitzvahs, and have sat shiva with my good friend when his daughter died. It was my honor and privilege to put my arm around Mike when his beloved daughter committed suicide. I prayed for the healing of his broken heart. I expressed my love to him and to his family even though we have different beliefs. I have even celebrated Ramadan with Muslim friends and have gotten along even with those who profess to be atheists. Even as I write this book one of the editors of my first book which deals with my acceptance of Jesus Christ has related to me that she is an atheist and does not believe as I do that Jesus Christ is the savior of the world. On the other hand, she is a good editor and has contributed to the success of my book. It is my hope that even this atheist editor might find some encouragement in the words that I have written because it is my duty to follow the commands of my savior to go into the all the world and to teach and baptized those who are in need of Jesus. Who then needs of Jesus? The answer is very clear, everyone!

Because humans are social animals, and because in the eyes of God we are all made in His image, He calls on all of His people, to love and care for everyone that we meet. I am required to show compassion to those in need, and mercy even to those who may have wronged me. I am called upon to fulfill Jesus's message to the young lawyer who asked Jesus "How shall I inherit eternal life?" The answer, that Christians hear from Jesus, is that we must not ignore those in need: whether that need is physical, mental or spiritual. If we have that mindset, we truly have fellowship, not only with our fellow human beings, but also with God.

Chapter 7
Forgive Me As I Forgive Those Who Trespass Against Me

In the Lord's Prayer (Matthew 6: 9-13, and Luke 11:2-4) Jesus tells us to pray as follows, "And forgive us our trespasses as we forgive those who trespass against us..." I believe what Jesus is telling us is that if we want to be forgiven by God, then we must also be forgiving to those who have wronged us. Why are we required to be so forgiving? The simple answer is because that is the very nature of God and if we wish to be godly, take on the attributes of God, we must be forgiving people.

How hard is it to be forgiving people? It is very hard. Our very nature, and often our first instinct, is that we seek revenge rather than mercy. When someone steps on our toes we are prone to step on their toes too. When we were in elementary school, if somebody pushed us down, we would get up and push them right back. I am prone to yell at people while I am driving if they do, what I refer to as, stupid stuff. I have told my wife that I am aware that people call each other in the night to plan how they can get in my way as I am driving to work in the morning. I know that they are doing that because I know that people just do not act that intentionally stupid unless they have planned it in advance to slow me down. I am being somewhat facetious of course. I do not really think that people stay up at night in order to figure out how to irritate me while I'm driving. On the other hand, I am prone to get angry and be unforgiving when things do not go my way.

Clearly, Jesus teaches us to be forgiving. In the Sermon on the Mount, at Matthew 5:38-45, Jesus says that in the Old Testament teaching was "an eye for an eye and a tooth for a tooth", but we are to not resist evil. If someone hits us on the right cheek, we are to turn to that person our left cheek. Further, if we get sued and they take away our coat we are supposed to give them our hat and scarf also. Further, if someone who has authority over us requires us to do an act that we do not like, we are supposed to do it to the fullest and without grumbling.

Jesus tells us that loving our neighbors is just not enough, we are also to bless those who think badly of us. Astonishingly, Jesus says at Matthew 5:44, "Love your enemies (let alone those who cut you off in traffic), bless them that curse you, do good to them that hate you, and pray for them which despitefully use you and persecute you; That you may be children of your Father which is in heaven; for He makes the sun to rise on the evil and on the good, and He sends the rain on the just and the unjust. If you love only them that love you back, what reward have you? Do not even the politicians do the same?" Then even more astonishingly, Jesus says at verse 48, "Be perfect just like God."

It is very interesting to me that Jesus talks about perfection in the context of loving our enemies. I think that before we were saved, we too were enemies of God. That part of us that is still under the control of Satan stands in opposition to our heavenly Father and we are at odds with being subject to God's will. Take for example our old friend Paul. Paul was a very religious man. He studied law under the best teachers in Jerusalem. He knew the law backwards and forwards and could probably quote long passages of the Old Testament. Paul thought that he was doing exactly what God had in mind when the law was given to Moses. How surprised he must have been, when Jesus told him that he was going in the exact wrong direction. Paul had to learn that it was not the enforcement of Jewish law that was important, it was keeping the love of God in his heart and passing it on to others that was the criteria for success in the eyes of God.

It boils down to, if God is a merciful God, and I expect God to show mercy to me, then I must have the godly attribute of being merciful to all those to whom God also shows mercy. To whom does God show mercy? God is merciful to all of us all the time. I need mercy all the time. You already know that I am somewhat intolerant of people in the morning and afternoon traffic. It is not as though I have never made a mistake while driving. There have been a few times when people have held up one of their fingers to me because I have done something stupid while I was driving. I probably need more mercy from those with whom I share the road than I should expect. Thank goodness that God does not meet out mercy to only those who are perfect. God shows mercy to anyone that will accept His son and seek forgiveness. God loves those who repent, and He is willing to show mercy and love because of our acceptance of Jesus.

How do we cultivate an ability to be merciful? I must say that we are not born with a spirit of mercy. We can only develop the spiritual gift of showing mercy by accepting Jesus into our lives and being sealed by the Holy Spirit. Paul says that when I was a child I acted just like a child. It is only when I became mature that I was able to see how silly I was in acting. Some of us never stop acting childishly; that is a real problem for many of us. Because it is not in our nature to be forgiving it is often a real struggle to reach that point of maturity that allows us to love our enemies and to pray for those who use us.

Paul in Philippians 4:6-8, writes, "Be careful about nothing; but in everything by prayer and supplication with thanksgiving let your request be made known unto God. And the peace of God, which passes all understanding, shall keep your hearts and minds through Christ Jesus. Finally whatsoever things are true, whatsoever things are honest, whatsoever things are just, whatsoever things are pure, whatsoever things are lovely, whatsoever things are of good report; if there be any virtue, if there be any praise, think on these things." Paul is telling us to fill our minds and souls with only good stuff, and if we do that, then only good stuff will come out of us. You ask, is it possible to only think of good things? It is very hard to do in the world we live in today.

Remember when we were talking about the parable concerning the sower of seeds? In that parable Jesus warns those that were listening to His preaching, and especially His disciples, that some of the seeds were inevitably going to land in the briar patch, and that the cares of the world choke the seed out, so that the words of the Gospel would be unproductive. I realized that every generation thinks that the distractions that they are encountering are the most difficult ever encountered by humans. However, today there are so many distractions that it is hard to tell a distraction from reality. Television, smart phones, computers on which you can pull up just about anything we may want view or hear surround us. These are such distractions that have never been seen or heard of before.

How then can we go about filling our hearts and minds with those good and pure things that Paul talks about in Philippians? Do we throw away our TV's, smartphones, and computers? Try living without a smartphone or a computer if you have work to do. If it was not for this computer, that I am using at this moment, it would be very hard for me to put these words together. We use smartphones in order to communicate good news and to keep up with those that we love. We can use almost anything for a good purpose or for bad purposes. It is therefore what is in your heart, mind, soul and with the strength that God has given us that we either choose to fill ourselves with good or with evil. If we are a child of God, we are protected from evil. If we are living a Christian life, we choose to see the good in people rather than condemn anyone that does not meet our standards. Is it not true that actions speak louder than words? How we treat others is an important part of our Christianity. Jesus clearly says that we are too do unto others as we would have them do unto us. (Matthew 7: 12)

William Barclay in his commentary regarding Jesus's pronunciation of the Golden Rule, says that that commandment from Jesus is perhaps the high point of the Sermon on the Mount. If we go about our daily lives as if we were living our lives in the presence of God and seek to treat everyone with whom we come in contact, with respect and humility, we take on some of the qualities of Jesus life and qualities that He demands for us to adopt. Forgiveness is at the heart of doing unto others as we would have them do to us. We are naturally imperfect until we are sealed with the Holy Spirit. If while I was in that imperfect state, I could be forgiven because it is God's desire to have a close fellowship with me then I too must be a forgiving person so that I can be godlier.

Chapter 8
People That Have Pure Hearts

Have you ever met somebody that you just knew, from the start, was going to be as honest as the day is long and you could trust them with everything that you own? Those kinds of people are rare but extremely good to find. Jesus says that people like that are extremely blessed. Jesus referred to such people as those that posse a pure heart. Jesus said those kinds of people will be able to see God. The way life is today not many people will be able to see God because there are not many that are pure at heart. We Christians should be pure, honest, trustworthy, kind and loyal. Those are the characteristics of a person that has a pure heart.

Doctors tell us that heart disease is often related to stress. If our lives are full of stress, it affects the function of our heart. For many years I practiced law and was subject to a stressful lifestyle. Eventually I had heart problems. In 2005 I was diagnosed with ventricular tachycardia also referred to as a v tach. A v tach is a condition in which your heartbeats so fast that it quits pumping blood to the rest of your body. In many instances it is fatal.

I had been in court that morning and was coming back to my office in Decatur, Georgia when my heart started racing. I became very dizzy and disoriented. I had to lean up against a telephone pole in order to keep from falling into the street. I finally made it to my office and the receptionist took one look at me and said, "You need to go to the emergency room." I let her drive my car with me as a passenger. We drove to the emergency entrance, and I got out and went in. I told the lady at the reception desk that my heart was beating really fast, and I was very dizzy. The next thing I knew I was on a gurney and was in a room, hooked up to an intravenous drip and with the doctor standing over me. The doctor told me that if my heart did not quit racing within a minute or two, he was going to put the electric paddles on me to shock my heart back into rhythm. I started to say something to the doctor, and he told me to be quiet because I was about to die. Surely, stress was one of the big factors for the heart problem that I was experiencing.

Having a pure heart is undoubtedly a cure for heart disease. Having a pure heart keeps us functioning the way God intended. In the Ten Commandments, we are told not to bear false witness. False witness is the same thing as lying. Lying causes stress; stress causes heart disease. Earlier in this book, I related that even as children we are prone to tell lies. Even though God told the children of Israel that they were not to bear false witness, God eventually had to punish His chosen people because they had become a nation of liars.

In the book of Amos in the Old Testament, the prophet warns Israel of the punishment of God that is about to be visited on the Israelites. The prophet says, "For as much therefore as you are treading is upon the poor, and you take from him burdens of wheat: You have built houses of hewn stone, but you shall not dwell in them; You have planted pleasant vineyards, but you shall not drink wine from them for I know your manifold transgressions and your mighty sins: they afflict the just, they take a bribe, they turn aside the poor in the gate from their right; therefore, the prudent shall keep silence in that time for it is an evil time. Seek good, and not evil, that he may live; so, the Lord the God of host shall be with you as you have spoken. Hate the evil; love the good and establish judgment in the gate; it may be that the Lord God of host will be gracious unto the remnant of Joseph." (Amos 5:11-15) What Amos is warning the children of Israel about is that their lifestyles have become inconsistent with righteousness. People have become obsessed with materialism at the expense of the poor. The wealthy were good at lying not only to the poor but also to themselves. The wealthy considered it a blessing from God that they were able to live in palaces and eat the best foods and wear the latest fashions. They were able to do this at the expense of the poor and that led to their ultimate downfall. Their wealth had become an idol.

There is really nothing wrong with trying to make an honest living and trying to provide the best for our families. However, when we become obsessed with money and all that money can buy, especially at the expense of those less fortunate, we are in danger of God's punishment. The children of Israel learned it the hard way. After they had been warned time and time again, that there was impending doom because of the way they were treating the poor and because they were not putting God first, (worshipping idols) they were forced into exile in Babylon. The exile lasted for approximately 80 years. It was not until those that suffered God's punishment, returned to serving God that their exile ended.

I told you that I experienced heart disease in the form of ventricular tachycardia. I mentioned that I had been under a good deal of stress as a result of my law practice. (I was also experiencing problems in my marriage which is a topic for another book, see Step by Step, Marriage, Law, Spiritual Warfare & the Holy Spirit.) When I eventually wound up in the hospital and had to have a defibrillator inserted into my chest, I became very depressed. I remember shortly after going into the hospital, in the night when I should have been sleeping, I began to cry uncontrollably. I realized that I was never going to be the same person again. I knew that there was going to be great changes in my life. I did not know what was going to become of me. Would I be able to continue practicing law? Would I be able to support myself and my family the way that I had been for the last 30 years?

When I got to that state of depression, I felt the presence of Jesus. I prayed that Jesus would allow me to change my life in such a way that it was more pleasing to Him. I felt an assurance that God would be with me even as I lay there in the hospital bed at DeKalb General Hospital in October of 2005.

The next day I had to take a stress test to determine whether there was any damage to my heart. There was none. A day or so later, I was taken to Piedmont hospital in Atlanta to have an MRI. They determined that I have occlusions on my left ventricle that cause the tachycardia. Because of that I had to undergo surgery to have a defibrillator placed in my chest. The defibrillator was placed by a doctor from the Ivory Coast of Africa.

A day or two later I had to return to the hospital to make sure that the defibrillator was working properly and was adjusted correctly. When I went back into the operating room, the doctor told me that I had a "screw loose." Because he was from Africa his accent was different and his sequence of words were different. When he told me, I had a "screw loose," I looked at him and told him that other people had told me that I had a loose screw. He said, "No, no I must open you up again and tighten your screw." Now when people tell me that I have a loose screw, I tell them, "No, I have been tightened up."

Could my tachycardia have been my Damascus Road experience? I certainly felt that I had undergone a life changing experience. It is true that I had felt another life changing experiences earlier when my first child was born, and I have felt other life changing experiences after I experienced the issues with my heart. I believe that these experiences are calls to me to be more faithful in my service to God. I never felt that God had left me or forsaken me. I have always known that I am saved and that I belong to His Kingdom since I gave myself to Jesus at that vacation Bible school in Hopkinsville, Kentucky more than 60 years ago. Each time I feel like my life is changing, I have reached out to God and have asked Him to take complete charge of my life. During those times I have felt that God has honored me by allowing me to feel His presence and His comfort.

Have I completed my Damascus Rd experiences? I do not think so. My heart still remains broken in many places. There are still loose screws in me that require tightening. That is to say that I do not believe that I have accomplished having a completely pure heart. I am still a work in progress, and it is my hope and prayer that my heart will become more pure so that one day I can see God.

Chapter 9
The Role of a Peacemaker

There has been a lot in the news this year concerning police and their proper function in society. Back in the 90s there was the trial of the police officers that were caught on camera beating Rodney King. After the police officers were determined to be not guilty, that set off a huge backlash in African American communities. More recently, peaceful protests resulted in outbreaks of violence that have occurred in many sections of the United States in both big cities and small towns. A recording of the murder of George Floyd on a cell phone by a teenage girl, set off weeks of protests under the banner of Black Lives Matter. In some cases, there were outraged individuals who took matters into their own hands. Today the police officer who was found guilty of the murder of George Floyd by a Minneapolis jury has been sentenced to a term in prison. Some are fearful that more riots may occur when the sentencing is announced. There has been mass shootings, riots, and political unrest in the United States even while we have been amid the coronavirus pandemic.

In the Sermon on the Mount, (Matthew 5: 9) Jesus said, "Those who are peacemakers will be extremely blessed and they shall be called the children of God." (My Paraphrase) Therefore, if you want to be called a child of God, and that is something that we should all strive for, we should always try to be people who bring about peace, not only with those around us, but throughout the world.

What are the characteristics of peacemakers and how do we take on the task of keeping the peace? Is it not in our national interest that peace reigns throughout the world? The United States spends vast amounts of money in its defense budget for the stated purpose of keeping peace. Often, our government uses its superior military advantage for the purpose of inducing other governments not to go to war. However, a show of might by governments has had the opposite effect on other belligerent nations.

Jesus says that in the end times nation will rise against nation and there will be wars and rumors of wars as a prelude to Jesus's return. (See Matthew 21, also referred to as the Olivet discourse). As a sign of the troubled age to come, Jesus warns His disciples that people will be out to kill them, persecute them, and His followers will be hated in all nations because of our faith in Christ. After all, Jesus says that the world hated Him first, so why should followers of Christ expect to be treated differently from our savior who admonishes us to take up our cross and follow Him.

Such warnings could cause Christians to take on an "us versus them" mentality. However, Christians are to be accepting of even those that we do not get along with, to the point of loving our enemies and doing good to those that persecute us. Clearly, Jesus put an emphasis on the Christian attitude that makes us people who really care about those with whom we come in contact. Paul tells us that peace comes from God. At Philippians 4:4-7, Paul says, "Rejoice in the Lord always: and again, I say, rejoice. Let your moderation be known unto all men. The Lord is at hand. Be careful about nothing; but in everything by prayer and supplication with thanksgiving let your request be made known unto God and the peace of God which passes all understanding, shall keep your hearts and minds through Christ Jesus."

Jesus says you are blessed if you are a peacemaker and that if you are a peacemaker, you will be the children of God. Paul says that we are to act in such a manner that the peace of God which comes through Christ Jesus will fill our hearts and minds. Even in today's turbulent world, which seems bent on self-destruction, peace can reign if God's Son is at the forefront of our thoughts and prayers. Paul had the mindset that Jesus was close by. After all, Jesus paid Paul a visit when I suppose Paul was least expecting such a visit. When Jesus called Paul to quit going in the wrong direction on the road to Damascus, it was not just a one-time visit by Jesus to Paul. From that time on Paul had a lifetime adventure with Jesus.

I believe that every morning when Paul got up, he expected a new word from Jesus. Before the sun went down every day, Paul knew that Jesus was a reality. Paul's life became dedicated to gaining a better understanding of what a relationship with Jesus would cause. While Paul experienced suffering as a result of his commitment to Jesus, he was beaten, stoned, chased out of town on several occasions, was shipwrecked, imprisoned and ultimately martyred, Paul still could say that by knowing Jesus that there was a peace that passed all his understanding because Jesus opened a continuing dialogue with Paul. Jesus can and will do the same for me and you. If we reach out to Jesus, He will fill our hearts and minds with the Holy Spirit, and we will become peacemakers.

Peace comes from God. Jesus who came from God, is the Prince of Peace. If we want to have true peace and be the instruments of that peace, we must have Jesus. I believe that there is no real peace without Jesus. Jesus statement at Matthew 5:9 was, therefore, absolutely true. When we take Jesus into our hearts and have an intimate relationship with Him, we are peacemakers and because we know Jesus, we are God's children. If you want to be blessed and be a peacemaker, initiate a relationship with Jesus today and a peace which is incomprehensible will be within your reach.

Persecutions may come, you will experience hatred, you may not even be accepted by many people that you admire, but you will have the adventure of your life. Jesus experienced persecution and hatred. Even though, He was equal to God, He gave up His place in heaven, became a man, became a servant, endured cruelty, suffered the agony of the cross, died and was buried but rose again on the third day and now sits at the right hand of God. Jesus tells us that we must also take up our cross and follow Him. If we do follow Jesus, we will be peacemakers and we will be part of the family of God now and forever more.

Chapter 10
Don't Worry Be Happy

A few years ago, there was a very popular song by Bobby McFerrin that was entitled, "Don't Worry Be Happy." I was fortunate enough to see the song performed by Mr. McFerrin at the Atlanta Symphony. The lyrics to the song were simple but the message could have been taken right out of the 6th chapter of Matthew. As a part of the Sermon on the Mount, Jesus tells His followers at verse 25, "Therefore, I tell you, do not worry about your life, what you will eat or drink or about your body, or what you will wear." Jesus goes on to point to the birds and tells his followers to take notice that birds neither sow nor reap but God takes care of them. Jesus also tells His followers to consider the flowers in the field and how beautiful they are. He reminds them that flowers do not worry about how they look because God has taken care of that. Jesus says that if God takes care of birds and flowers, He will also take care of us.

Anxieties are normal until they become obsessive. We all worry about whether we will pass the test. We worry if we will meet the right person to marry. We may even worry about whether we are appropriately dressed for the party to which we have been invited. We may be anxious about a job interview or even whether we are overdrawn on our bank account. These issues are normal, and we do not normally become obsessed with these daily parts of our lives. However, when our worries and anxieties take over our lives and we cannot function in a normal manner, then we must seek help.

We have just gone through a tough year in 2020 and it has carried over into 2021 too. The Covid Virus (and now the variants of the original strain) pandemic has changed our lives. The November 2020, presidential election has been a source of great controversy throughout The United States. People say that there is a new normal as a result of what we have gone through. The old normal depended on who you are and where you live and is somewhat hard to determine. What the new normal will be is equally hard to determine. Such dramatic change in the way that people interact, think about their lives, and go about their daily routine can cause extreme anxiety. I find myself wandering when I will be able to feel comfortable around others. Do I need to wear a mask all the time from now on? Will the vaccination that I received a few months ago protect me from the new variants that are being discussed in the media?

There are many things to be concerned about as we go into the post pandemic era. I am sure many people are greatly troubled by the dramatic changes that have gone on over the last two years. In the Sunday school class that I am now teaching, the men seem very concerned about the direction of the government. They often express how worried they are concerning the direction of the current leadership and express their anxiety about the future.

Those that have suffered from an anxiety disorder, prior to all the turmoil that has gone on in recent times, may find it necessary to seek help from mental health professionals. I have read articles in magazines and in the newspapers that I follow, that indicate that anxiety is especially prevalent in younger women. I pray on a regular basis for those that I know that suffer from anxiety attacks that they will find solace in the words of Jesus and that I may try to be of help.

I am not a mental health professional, and it is very difficult for me to understand the root causes of anxiety and abnormal worry. I want to be of help to those around me who suffer from these debilitating anxiety attacks. One night my closest friend suffered an anxiety attack while we were together. She had physical symptoms of shortness of breath and heart palpitation. I felt helpless to help her overcome what was something that I had never experienced before. She asked me to pray with her. We held hands and I prayed that the anxiety that she was feeling would go away and that her a feeling of well-being would be restored to her. We prayed for many hours that night. I wish I could say that my prayer for her totally alleviated her symptoms, but it did not. I believe that it did help but she still suffers anxiety from time to time and when she does my heart is broken for her and I continue to pray almost every day that God will relieve her of these feelings.

One of my closest friends, Mike Froman, believes that all mental disorders result from a chemical imbalance in the body. Today's medical treatment of many psychological problems result in the prescription of drugs that are designed to bring about a balance of those chemicals in the brain that are known to cause certain reactions in humans. Mike believed that his daughter could be successfully medicated with the drugs that were prescribed for her and that her anxieties and depressions would be alleviated. It was a matter of getting the right amount of the drug into her to reach the right balance in her system.

It did seem that as though the chemical imbalance from which Mike's daughter suffered had been successfully treated and that she was on the road to recovery. Mike's daughter graduated from college, she met a man that loved her; she was married, and she had a beautiful daughter of her own. Then tragedy struck, one morning, my very close friend was in very deep grief. His daughter had committed suicide. She evidently could not overcome the anxiety and depression from which she had suffered for many years. Mike's grief overwhelmed me. Because the Froman family is Jewish, burial had to take place the next day, and because it was suicide, she could not be buried in the Jewish section of the cemetery.

With these two experiences, with my closest friend and with my experience with Mike, how can I accept the Instruction of Jesus and even Paul for that matter, of "do not worry and be anxious for nothing?" It is hard to see your friends and your loved one's suffering from what they believe to be a chemical imbalance or psychological problems without trying to figure out how we as Christians can completely ignore the fact that anxiety exists and that mental health issues that stem from anxiety, fear, and depression are prevalent. Therefore, a closer look at the words of Jesus found in Matthew 6:25-34 is necessary.

Remember before we considered this passage from Matthew 6, when it came to Jesus telling his followers that they exhibited "little faith". This is a part of the Sermon on the Mount discourse that Matthew records. This part of the sermon is sandwiched between "laying up treasures in heaven" and Jesus's admonition that we should not judge others.

Jesus tells those who were listening to the sermon that His followers should not worry about what they were going to eat, drink, or clothes they would be wearing. Jesus points to the bird and says that they do not sow or reap or put things in barns and yet God takes care of them. Jesus then points to the flowers in the field and says they are beautiful the way they are without the need of labor or spinning. Jesus points out that the flowers are only temporary, here today gone tomorrow. From this, I believe Jesus is saying God has my back and therefore it is not necessary for me to become overly concerned about material things. Further, Jesus tells me that I have little faith when I do not recognize God's hand in even these aspects of my life.

Jesus says pagans who do not believe in God spend their time worrying and have anxiety concerning physical necessities. We as Christians, however, should have the ability to rely on God because if God knows what the birds need and how to dress the flowers, He surely knows the needs of those of His higher creation. Then, in the climax of this passage, Jesus tells those who are listening to seek first the Kingdom of God, because by seeking God first the things that you need, the things that God already knows that you need, will be given to you as well. Then you do not have to worry about today, because today will take care of itself and each day has enough trouble of its own.

Immediately after that passage, Jesus says, "do not judge others or you will be also judged." Because if you judge others, you well be judged by the same standard by which you are judging. Can it be that anxiety and fear come from how we think people perceive us. If we are judgmental, are we not really judging our own selves? If we see ourselves as not being up to the standards we set for others, do we not also become anxious that our faults will be revealed. When we see our own faults and compare ourselves with others, we are bound to become anxious and fearful that others might also see the faults that we recognize in ourselves. Therefore, Jesus's admonition to seek God's Kingdom and His righteousness first will have two immediate benefits.

First, we will see ourselves as God sees us. We are His perfect creation. No matter how we look, or are dressed, we are made in the image of God and therefore we are perfect in His eyes. We do not have to judge ourselves by the human standards to which we have become accustomed. It does not matter if I am wearing the latest fashion or hand me downs. God does not look at us with human eyes but with spiritual eyes. If our emphasis is on being pleasing to God, we should not care about our perceptions of others. In other words, the object is not to look at ourselves (becoming an existentialist) but to understand that I am God's creation and to look towards God who already knows everything I need and is willing and able to supply all that I need.

Secondly, my focus will not be on myself or others. my focus will be on God. When I give myself the opportunity to communicate, in fellowship with my Creator, I will have a peace that passes all understanding. That peace comes from a knowledge and belief that God truly loves me, and that I belong to Him. Knowing that we belong to our Creator, regardless of our current circumstance, generates in us a powerful feeling of acceptance. When we feel accepted there is no longer a need to be judgmental of others or of ourselves. We go from having a focus on our physical needs to having spiritual eyes and we will see beyond any physical or even emotional disabilities that we think we may have.

Jesus in the book of Revelations, sends letters to seven churches in Asia Minor. In each of His letters, Jesus tells the churches that, "Whoever has ears, let them hear what the Spirit says to the churches." From that I perceive that in order to hear what the Holy Spirit has to say, the message must be heard with spiritual ears. By this I mean, if we are to understand what Jesus tells His churches, which are made up of people like us, we must be listening with a sense of the spirit who dwells within us. We must follow the leadership of the Holy Spirit as it moves within us. If the Holy Spirit is not within us, it is impossible to hear what Jesus needs us to hear.

The Holy Spirit is also referred to, by Jesus, as the Comforter. Evidently, in order for us to be comforted by the Holy Spirit we must be possessed by that same Holy Spirit. To be possessed by the Holy Spirit requires that we commit ourselves to Jesus Christ. When we are committed to Jesus Christ and the Holy Spirit dwells in us, we can fully give up anxiety, worry, fear and depression. We then have an extraordinary source of comfort, peace, and acceptance on which we can always rely.

Is it possible to live a life in which there is no worries, and we are happy all the time? Bobby McFerrin sang that we should "don't worry, be happy" but only Jesus Christ can make it happen. If you are happy in your spirit, that happiness will change your emotional status. If your emotional status is balanced your physical needs will be met. If you are still anxious, you have not found the love of Christ and you should seek it now.

Chapter 11
Asking, Seeking, Knocking

As a part of my personality, I am always asking questions. It was probably that questioning personality that others recognized in me when I was a child that made people tell me that I should be a lawyer. Sometimes it would get me in trouble, I would question my mother's instructions. I wanted to know why I had to have shots. My mother wanted to fool me into believing that we were not going to the Navy base for me to see the doctor and to get a shot. She told me, "We are just going for a ride." But as soon as we got to a certain street and turned onto the Navy base, I knew that I was going to have to endure sitting in the waiting room, at the base clinic, with who knows how many other screaming fidgeting children and endure my shots. Generally, I sat in the back of our green 1952 Plymouth automobile and when I knew for certain that it was shot time for me, I would scoot all the way across the seat and as far away from my mother as possible.

Mother was undeterred. She would open the back door of the car, reach across the seat, grab me by my foot, and drag me out of the car. She continued to drag me up the stairs to the clinic, and finally into the waiting room with all those other screaming children. I was going to get my shot whether I wanted it or not. Of course, mother probably had my best interest at heart, but try telling that to a 6- or 7-year-old child who questioned his mother's motives from the start. I questioned mother's motives because I did not understand that it was really in my best interest to be fully vaccinated from such diseases as whooping cough, tetanus, measles, mumps, polio, and tuberculosis. (I am sure if my mother were alive today, she would be happy that I have received my

COVID shot. Even though down deep it was my belief that mother took me to get shots only to torture me.)

By the time I got to college I was very good at asking relevant questions. Even when I was a freshman, my college professors would seek me out after class to tell me that the questions that I asked in class were always on point and provided a basis for a better understanding for the entire class. After law school, I was given the privilege to ask questions as a part of my profession. You might say then that I became a paid questioner. Even with all the experience that I have had about asking questions, none of that is really on point when it comes to Jesus telling those who were listening to His sermon that they should ask, and it will be given to them. Matthew 7:7.

Is Jesus really giving us a blank check so that we can ask whatever we want and receive payment in full? I do not know about you, but it does not seem to work that way for me. When I was a child and would go to see my grandmother, in the summer, we at times would go fishing in her pond that was in the backyard of her house. We would fish and invariably my patience would wear out and I would complain that the fish did not want to be caught that day. Grandma would say, "You are not holding your mouth right." Of course, holding your mouth in any particular position had nothing to do with whether the fish decided to be caught or not. The point that I think that I am trying to make is, Jesus is not impressed with a method of asking, or even what our request may be (after all, God already knows our needs). I believe that if we are motivated by what God wants then we can ask for anything and it will be given to the furtherance of His Kingdom.

In Matthew 7:8 Jesus says, "For anyone who asks receives; The one who seeks finds; And the one who knocks, the door will be opened." The question that I have is, who shall we ask? Where shall we seek? And on whose door should I be knocking? While it seems obvious that Jesus is talking about asking God, seeking God and knocking on heaven's door, I think it is worthwhile exploring this passage from the Sermon on the Mount to get some insight into exactly what we are expected to ask for, seek, and learn how to determine which door it is that we want to have opened.

Let us go back a little to the Beatitudes and see the kind of people that Jesus recognizes as being blessed. Jesus starts out at Matthew 5:3 by saying, "Blessed are the poor in spirit, for theirs is the Kingdom of heaven." William Barclay in his commentary on that verse translate blessed to mean extremely fortunate. You might ask how is it extremely fortunate to be poor in spirit? Again, Barclay says that a person is poor in spirit when they are totally reliant on someone. In this case, a person is extremely fortunate if he is totally reliant on God. A person who is totally reliant on God is someone that has faith that God will supply all his needs. So, when Jesus says that we are to ask, what he is saying is that a person who is totally reliant on God should ask God and God will supply such good gifts as are necessary to promote that person's faith.

Jesus in that same passage in Matthew 7 expounds on what kind of gifts are likely to be given. Jesus says, if your child asks you for a loaf of bread, do you give that child a stone? If your child asks for a fish, do you give that child a snake? Then Jesus says if you who are evil, know how to give good gifts to your children, how much more likely is it that God will give you good gifts because He is abundantly good? James tells us that all good gifts come from God. James 1:17

What kind of gifts does God give to believers? We have previously discussed the spiritual gifts that we are entrusted with by the Holy Spirit. Some of those gifts are the ability to preach or teach or the gift of hospitality. (See our discussion of spiritual gifts in Chapter 3) In order to understand these gifts, take a quick look at Matthew 6:19-24. In that passage Jesus tells those that are listening not to store up treasures on earth because earthly treasures are subject to theft, rust, and corruption; but only to store up treasures in heaven that are permanent and will never pass away.

Jesus plainly says in verse 24, "You cannot serve both God and money." Therefore, it is quite clear that God does not consider money a good gift. (Although, the song lyrics to the rock and roll classic, Money says it best, "There are many things that can cure your ills, but only one thing that can pay your bills.") Because God only gives good gifts, we should take into consideration the good gifts that God is willing to give us. Those gifts are heavenly. When we ask for those gifts, God gives to us liberally.

What then shall I seek? The book of Psalms on a regular basis tells us that God provides gifts to those who diligently seek Him. In Hebrews 11:6 the scripture writer tells us that, "Without faith it is impossible to please God, because anyone who comes to Him must believe that He exists and that He rewards those who earnestly seek Him." Therefore, if you want to receive a reward from God, you must believe that God well hear your request and that if your request earnestly seeks to do God's will, God will honor that request and reward you.

How do you earnestly (diligently) seek God? The simple answer is through prayer and Bible study. Jesus prayed. The apostles prayed. Paul prayed. A few years ago, I traveled to Seville, Spain. In Seville there is a cathedral that contains the bones of Christopher Columbus. The church is very old and is said to be the third largest Catholic cathedral in the world. One Sunday morning I got up and was in need of prayer and I ventured into that Catholic cathedral in Seville, Spain. The priest as part of the Catholic tradition, burned incense during the ceremony. The smoke from the incense rose towards the roof of the cathedral and it just happened that the ceiling was very high. It reminded me of all the prayers that must have been said in that immense Catholic Church over the past centuries. Christians pray. The manner in which we pray is between us and our Lord. The importance of prayer is that we diligently seek and when we do, we shall find.

Knocking is a sign of our understanding that we are seeking entrance that requires an invitation. If I go to my own house I don't knock before I enter. However, if I am going even to my friend's house, I generally knock on the door to make sure that my friend at least has his/her clothes on. Even when I am invited and am expected, it is just polite to knock. When I am seeking entrance into the presence of God I must come with reverence. Even if I have an expectation that I am welcome, and that God is expecting me, I must ask God's permission to enter into His presence. Jesus says, if you knock with that kind of a spirit of reverence, the door will be open, and God will graciously receive you.

Lastly, Jesus tells His listeners at Matthew 7:12 that we are to do unto others as we would want them to do to us. The Hebrew rabbis were willing to concede that you should not do anything to even strangers that you would not want them to do to you. The statement of Jesus goes much beyond that legalistic approach. Jesus words require that we take the first step in seeking to advance God's Kingdom. We are not to refrain from doing what we do not want done to us; we are to positively do for others what we expect to have done for our well-being. If we are doing for others, treating them, as we want to be treated, we take the positive first step. We do not sit back and let the world come to us, we act proactively.

If I know that I want to have something good to eat, and I see someone that is without, Jesus requires that I feed them with something good to eat. When I do this to the least of those around me, I am doing it at the direction of and for Jesus. Jesus later says at Matthew 25, when you do these things to the least of these that you come across, you will be rewarded because you will have laid up treasure for yourself in heaven.

Chapter 12
Predestination or Free Will

At one time in my life, I was asked to be a part of an evangelistic team that traveled throughout the state of Georgia for the purpose of conducting lay led revivals. That group was made up of approximately 10 or 12 Christian men and women who agreed to travel to towns throughout the state and meet with local congregations beginning on Friday afternoon and lasting until after the noon day church service on Sunday.

In advance of our travel to the local churches, we asked the local church to provide a list of individuals that they believed needed salvation. When we got to the church, we generally had a fellowship meal with the congregation, followed by introductions, a time of prayer, and a brief orientation regarding the purpose of the weekend's events. We were always housed in the homes of members of the congregation.

On Saturday morning, we would meet at the church for a time in which our leader would provide instruction in how to approach people for the purpose of personal evangelism. That session lasted until around noon and entailed instruction on sharing the gospel with unsaved people. Team members would then pair up with someone from the local congregation for the purpose of going out into the community to witness and if possible, to lead those that would listen to us to Christ. After we had gone throughout the community, we would come back to the church in order to make a report of what had happened during our time of personal evangelism. On Sunday morning the team members were in charge of the church service and would often give their personal testimonies and other invitations to accept Jesus as personal savior.

In Ephesians 1:4 Paul tells us, "For He chose us in Him before the creation of the world to be holy and blameless in His sight. In love He predestined us for adoption to sonship through Jesus Christ in accordance with His pleasure and will, to the praise of His glory and grace, which He has freely given us in the one He loves." Also, at Romans 8:23 Paul says, "And we know that in all things God works for the good of those who love Him, who have been called according to His purpose. For those God foreknew He also predestined to be conformed to the image of His son that He might be the first born among many brothers and sisters and those He predestined, He also called; Those He called he also justified; Those He justified He also glorified."

You may ask, what do you mean by predestination? Predestination is defined, as a doctrine in Christian theology, of the divine foreordaining of all that will happen, especially with regard to the salvation of some and not others. It has been particularly associated with the teachings of Saint Augustine of Hippo and of John Calvin. We have had a brief discussion of Calvinism in the previous chapters of this book. In essence, the doctrine of predestination asserts that it does not matter what you do, God has either chosen you for salvation or not from the creation of the world. There is a branch of Baptists who are referred to as Primitive Baptist or Hard -Shell Baptist that follow Calvin's beliefs regarding predestination.

If we believe that God knows everything in advance, that He is omnipotent and all knowing, then we could rightly believe that predestination has already set-in, and we are either saved or not and we have no control of our ability to accept or reject Christ. That however tends to make us fatalistic. On the other hand, Jesus sent his disciples into the whole world for the purpose of being witnesses, teachers, preachers, and baptizing those who professed Jesus as their savior. Paul in 1 Timothy, tells us that God has called everyone to be saved. Therefore, if everyone is called to be saved, God has predestined everyone for salvation.

Is there a way to reconcile the idea of predestination with the idea that every man is capable of accepting Jesus Christ as their personal savior? When I was teaching a Sunday school class at Peachtree Baptist Church in Atlanta, one of the men in that class had grown up in a Primitive Baptist tradition. He would often express his belief that one could not know whether they were saved until they met Jesus in heaven. That man would not express a knowledge of his salvation and it made him reluctant to profess his salvation to others. While I respected that man in my Sunday school class, I could not agree with him concerning his theology.

Jesus in Matthew 28:18 told his disciples, "All authority in heaven and on earth has been given to me. Therefore, go and make disciples of all nations, baptizing them in the name of the Father and of the Son and the Holy Spirit, teaching them to obey everything that I have commanded you. And surely, I am with you always, to the very end of the age." When Jesus said that we are to make disciples in all nations, and to baptize those who have become His disciples, I do not believe that He is saying that anyone should or could be left out of Jesus's call for salvation.

When I was a part of the ley lead revival group, it was my great pleasure to witness to people and to invite them to accept Jesus as their personal savior. There were several occasions when I saw the hand of God bringing salvation to people who had not previously made a profession of faith in Jesus. I recall on one occasion when I was in a small town in South Georgia, below the gnat line, that I went out with the specific purpose of evangelism. I was asked to go out with a church member to visit a family that lived way out in the country.

When we got to the house, we knocked on the door and no one, at first, came to answer our knock. We were about to leave and put a flyer on their door with a tract that offered salvation. We decided to knock one last time and to our surprise a child came to the door. We told the little girl that we wanted to see her parents and surprisingly she let us in. Before long, the mother asked us if we would like to sit at the breakfast table. Soon, other members of the family began to gather around. I asked if any of them had ever made a profession of faith in Jesus Christ, and they all denied that they had. I asked if it would be alright if I shared the plan of salvation with the family members. They agreed to listen to what I had to say. At the end I asked if anyone wanted to receive Jesus into their life? Right there at the breakfast table, and they all agreed. We prayed together. They all asked for forgiveness of their sins. Each one of them asked for Jesus to come into their heart and to save them.

I truly felt the movement of the Holy Spirit at that time and at that place. I asked the church member that was with me to follow up with that family and to make sure that they were given proper instruction concerning the profession of faith that they had just made and the discipleship that needed to go on from that time forward. It was truly a memorable day for me, and I hope for that family that received salvation from Jesus Christ that Saturday morning way out in the country in South Georgia.

Was that family predestined to have me knock on their door that morning? Could they not have refused to come to the door and let me and the man that was with me into their home? If it was not me would someone else have been able to be with them when they professed Christ? To be quite honest, I do not know. I like to think that because I chose to drive from Atlanta down to that town in South Georgia and chose to be a member of the ley lead revival team, that I made a difference in the lives of those members of that family.

What I do know is that Jesus gave me the desire, the opportunity, the training, and the ability to share the gospel message. Was my appearance at that door, in the country, in South Georgia, a Damascus Road experience for me and for the family that was home that morning. For me, I am very grateful. I believe it was the gift of God and that I will have a reward in heaven.

Chapter 13
Personal Evangelism

Advertising agents tell us that in order to sell to more people it is necessary to meet people on a personal basis. Mass marketing of products works to some extent but to a much lesser extent than "in person" sales. There are statistics devised by marketing experts that tell us how many sales we can expect from mass marketing and the number of sales that we can expect when the sales pitch is made in person. The insurance industry relies heavily on individual sales. I do not contend that personal evangelism is like making a sale. There are so many other factors in personal evangelism that must be taken into consideration, however, personal evangelism must be personal.

Alcoholics Anonymous is based on the principle that in order to overcome an addiction to alcohol the alcoholic has to come to a realization that his life is out of control and that he needs to rely on a higher power in order to overcome his addiction. The alcoholic has to come to a realization that he is powerless and that his life is out of control. Some people call that hitting the bottom. I have been to a few Alcoholics Anonymous meetings in support of people that I love. Alcoholics Anonymous is based on a "12 Step" program in which the alcoholic works through his addiction. The centerpiece of the Alcoholics Anonymous meetings are testimonies by those who are recovering from their addiction. Each of those that testify stand before the group and say, "Hello my name is _____, and I am an alcoholic." The admission of the alcoholic is the first step to recovery.

The members of Alcoholics Anonymous are encouraged to follow the "12 Step" program in order to overcome their addiction. Each of the participants has to admit that he / she is powerless and that he/she must rely upon the intervention of a higher power in order to overcome the addiction. Interestingly as part of the Alcoholics Anonymous program there is a book that is generally referred to as the "Big Book" that discusses the higher power but refuses to name who the higher power may be. The results of the Alcoholics Anonymous program are phenomenal.

In order to overcome addiction to alcohol or other addictive behaviors, including drug addiction, addiction to gambling, pornography, and many other types of addiction, an individual must come to a realization that he/she is powerless over the addiction and needs the help of a higher power to bring about a recovery from the addiction. (It is similar, to asking that your sins be forgiven but not exactly the same as repentance) Even though a "12 Step" program requires a recognition that there is a higher power that can enable an addicted person to overcome his addiction, a "12 Step" program is not the same thing as accepting Jesus Christ into your heart and becoming saved.

Jesus calls on us to be witnesses. Jesus does not tell us to go out and buy airtime on TV, or to take out ads in the newspaper or magazines in order to share the gospel. Jesus does tell us however, to share the gospel and to make disciples and to baptize. It occurs to me that Jesus is requiring each of us to become personal evangelists when we meet people who are unsaved. You may ask how can you do that? While there is no specific method by which any particular person can be saved, there is a general outline that I have used when trying to tell people what Jesus has done in my life. It is important that we as witnesses are able to relate our own personal experience with Jesus. A witness is a person who speaks from experience. Unless you have had a personal experience with Christ you cannot be a witness.

I must say from the start however, that no one can lead a person to Christ. Only the Holy Spirit has the power to convict a person that he/she is a sinner and of his/her need of salvation. We as Christians are only witnesses to what Christ has done in our lives. Therefore, whenever I encounter an individual and there is a possibility that I can share my faith with that person I first pray that the Holy Spirit will open the person that I am encountering to the realization that they are a sinner so that the conversation will result in that individual's recognition of their need for Jesus Christ.

When I was with the lay lead revival team, one of the last things that we did before going out into the community was to pray that the Holy Spirit would go in front of us, lead us to someone that was in need salvation, prepare the way for us to meet that person and to convict that person of their need to have Jesus enter their life.

In that regard, I offer the following suggestions as a general outline of how I approached someone with the good news that God loves them, and that He wants them to be saved. (1 Timothy 1:4-6, "Who will have all men to be saved, and to come unto the knowledge of the truth. For there is one God, and one mediator between God and man, the man Jesus Christ, who gave Himself a ransom for all, to be justified in due time."

1. I tried to establish a rapport with the person with whom I was meeting. I generally would strike up a conversation about anything that may be of interest in the news. Recently, there has been the condominium collapse in Seaside, Florida. I would say something like isn't it a tragedy that so many people have lost their homes and even their lives. That opening would lead me to a discussion of whether the loss of possessions could be covered by insurance. I would then try to bring the conversation around to whether the people that were caught in that catastrophe knew that they were about to meet God. I would then ask that person with whom I was having the conversation could they face God if something catastrophic were to happen to them today. If they said they were a believer in God and in Jesus I would move on to another topic. But if they said that they did not know what they would do or if they were saved then I would tell them of my own personal experience.

2. I would tell them that God loves me, and God loves them as well. I would tell them that God has offered me a full and meaningful life, and that He makes that offer to everyone including you. I would tell the person to whom I was talking that life without God's love is empty and without meaning. Jesus said, "I am come that they might have life, and they might have it more abundantly." John 10:10. I would say that my experience has been that when I am apart from Jesus my life has not been full and at times feels empty. But because God loves me, God wants me to have a life full of meaning and that He wants me to have a life with Him after my days on earth are over.

3. A full and meaningful life is possible through the death and resurrection of Jesus Christ. I would

say that I have experienced this and am experiencing a meaningful life because of my relationship with Jesus Christ. I would say that the Bible at Romans 5:8 says that "But God pronounces His love to us because, while we were sinners Christ died for us." And that, "Christ was delivered for our offences and was raised again for our justification." I would tell them that the death and resurrection of Jesus Christ was the method by which God has shown to us His love and desire for us to become a part of His family.

4. I would tell anybody that I was talking to that my life without Christ was characterized by guilt, loneliness, weariness and weakness, but that my life after my acceptance of Jesus is characterized by forgiveness (Romans 8:17), fellowship (Galatians 3:24), and strength (Philippians 4:19).

5. I would tell anybody who was listing to me that in order to receive Christ into their life that they must be born again. John 3:3 and 18. I would say this spiritual birth is more than an acceptance of facts (James 2:19) and is more than just doing good works (Ephesians 2:8-9). I would tell them that spiritual birth is the gift of God. A gift is not earned or purchased; a gift is an offer that only must be accepted. A spiritual birth occurs when you accept the gift of Jesus and realize that it is only through Jesus that you can have a full and meaningful life.

6. If the person was still there and listening to me, I would tell them that a failure to accept Jesus into their life is the ultimate sin. John 3:18. A life without Christ is the life of a sinner that is empty and meaningless but with Christ in your life, life becomes abundantly full, and you receive the gift of eternal life. Without Christ you are separated from God. Romans 6:23.

7. In order to accept Christ, I would tell my listener, it is necessary for you to admit that you are a sinner and ask Jesus to forgive you of your sins and agree to change your life. I would tell my listener that sin can be anything that is outside of the will of God. I would say that if you admit that you need Jesus, turn from your sins, and ask Jesus to take control of your life you will be saved and enter into the Kingdom of God. At that point if they agreed with me That they needed to accept Jesus, then I would ask them to pray as follows: "Heavenly Father, I admit that I am a sinner and that I am in need of Jesus. I turn away from my sins and ask Jesus to forgive me and take control of my life. Amen."

8. If that person prayed that prayer, I would tell this newly saved person that you have an assurance of eternal life because by calling on the name of Jesus you have been saved. Romans 10:13. The moment that you accepted Jesus you were sealed by His Holy Spirit and now you are in Jesus and Jesus is also in you. 1 John 4:13 and Romans 8:16.

If I had gotten that far with the person that I was talking to, I would tell them that it is important to grow in their knowledge and faith in Jesus Christ. I would tell them that it is necessary to pray and to study scripture. I would tell them that they should be baptized and join into a Christian fellowship where they will find people willing to help them with establishing a prayer life and teaching to them the word of God found in the Bible. Because of their newfound faith they would need to understand that God wants to provide them with spiritual gifts and that they will probably want to share those gifts and their salvation with others. I would also tell them that it would be my privilege to assist them in any way possible because they had just become my brother and sister in Christ.

What is your place in this call to be witnesses? In Matthew 10, Jesus sent out his disciples and gave them the command as to what they are supposed to do. They were not to go around the gentiles nor around the Samaritans, but they were to go to the lost sheep of Israel. (Jesus later modified His command by giving the Great Commission to go into all the world.) They were to proclaim the message that the Kingdom of heaven has come near. They were to heal the sick, raise the dead, cleanse those who had leprosy, and drive out demons. Jesus told them that they were given these powers freely and that freely they must use those powers. Just prior to sending out his disciples Jesus told them that the harvest is plentiful, but the workers are few. Jesus said to ask the Lord of the harvest to send out workers into the harvest field.

Is it not the same today? Do we not all know people who are in need? There are plenty of sick not only physically but mentally and especially spiritually. People are in need everywhere we turn. Everyone likes to put up a front that indicates everything is well, but we often know that people are hurting. The words of Jesus are correct, the needs are great (the harvest is plentiful) but there are few that will go into the fields to bring about healing.

It is our place as followers of Christ to heed the words that He gave to His disciples. We are to go, we are to seek, we are to ask those whose hearts are broken, we are to knock on doors of those who are in need. We are to tell our friends and neighbors that the Kingdom of heaven is at hand and that they too can enter as heirs and joint heirs in the family of God. We must tell everyone that God loves them and wants to have a fellowship with them. We must tell everyone that God exists and that He rewards those that diligently seeks Him. When we do that, we are obeying the commands of Jesus. if we do not follow Jesus's commands to go, seek and knock, we are neglecting His call to make disciples of all the world. If we are not about our Master's work, when He comes again and finds us neglecting His commands, there will be consequences. I do not think you would like the outcome of not following the commands of Jesus.

Jesus in His parable found in Matthew 13 says, "The one who sowed the good seed is the Son of Man. The field is the world, and the good seed stands for the people of the Kingdom. The weeds are the people of the evil one, and the enemy who sews them is the devil. The harvest is the end of the age, and the harvesters are angels. As the seeds are pulled up and burned in the fire so it will be at the end of the age. The Son of Man will send out His angels and they will weed out His Kingdom of everything that causes sin and all who do evil. They will throw them into the blazing furnace, where there will be weeping and gnashing of teeth. Then the righteous will shine like the sun in the Kingdom of their Father whoever has ears let them hear."

Refusing to comply with Jesus commands, is playing into the hands of the devil. As has been said, you cannot be in the Kingdom partially, if you are in the Kingdom of God, you will do the work that God has commanded you to do. If you do not, Jesus has already laid out the consequences. if you follow Jesus commands, you will be considered righteous and will shine like the sun. On the other hand, those who refuse to follow Jesus's commands will be thrown into a blazing furnace where there will be weeping and gnashing of teeth.

Chapter 14
Not All Who Call Me Lord Will Be Saved

While I am writing this book, I am thinking of who may be interested in reading it and if these words make any difference in the lives of my readers. It is certainly my hope and prayer that, you as my reader, will start to examine the Damascus Road experience in your life.

When we started this discussion, I stated that there could be positives and negatives in anybody's experiences that are life changing. Some of you even as you read this effort on my part to speak from my heart, will find it hard to accept. Others may find that my thoughts on my relationship with Jesus are absurd. Our old friend Paul said as much. In 1 Corinthians 1:18, Paul writing to the church at Corinth says, "For the message of the cross is foolishness to those who are perishing, but to us who are saved it is the power of God."

We Christians tend to hang with each other (that is we have fellowship with other Christians) We go to church on a somewhat regular basis. We participate in Sunday school, pray on regular basis, study our Bibles, are concerned for those in need, and seek to be witnesses to those who we know who are unsaved. Christians understand that there is a spiritual side to their life that is as important as their physical and emotional will being.

The unsaved not so much. We have all known people who are so self-centered that they are only concerned with what they have to the exclusion of everything and everyone else. There are others who may even be considerate and well mannered, but who do not care about the spiritual needs of those with whom they come in contact. Usually, those individuals are somewhat oblivious to their own spirituality. Such people may have a knowledge that Jesus was a historical figure and know the history of the church. At James 2:19 the author of that epistle says, "You believe that there is one God. Good! Even the demons believe that- and shudder."

In the Sermon on the Mount, Matthew 7:21-23, Jesus says, "Not everyone who says to me, 'Lord, Lord', will enter the Kingdom of heaven, but only the one who does the will of my Father who is in heaven. Many will say to me on that day, 'Lord, Lord, did we not prophesy in your name and in your name drive out demons, and in your name perform many miracles?' Then I will tell them plainly, 'I never knew you. Away from me you evil doers.'"

The criteria that Jesus lays out for His acceptance of us as His followers, certainly is not a head knowledge of Jesus nor even considering Jesus as a lucky charm. Jesus is looking for a spiritual awareness, a confession that He and He alone is the way, the truth, and the life; and that no man can come to God except through repentance, and a diligent seeking of Christ and the acceptance of His spirit within us. Jesus says, "Enter through the narrow gate. For wide is the gate and broad is the road that leads to destruction, and many will enter through it. But small is the gate and narrow the road that leads to life, and only a few find it." Matthew 7:13-14.

I have heard it said that the word used in this particular part of the scripture could be interpreted to be not a road but more like a funnel. If you look at a funnel, one end of it is small and we use the small end as the exit point for whatever we are trying to transfer from one vessel to another. The larger part of the funnel is usually the opening we pour the liquid that we are transferring to a smaller vessel. In this verse Jesus is telling us that it is very easy to get ourselves into the large portion of the funnel but very often that leads to destruction. Interestingly, right after Jesus's pronouncement about the narrow road is Jesus's warning that there will be true and false prophets.

Jesus tells us how to recognize a false prophet. He says you will know them by their fruit. Because I ask a lot of questions, I want to know for what fruit am I to look? Jesus explains that a good prophet Is like a good tree. A good tree only bears good fruit. On the other hand, a bad prophet can be recognized by the bad fruit that he/she produces.

What is good fruit and what is bad fruit especially from a spiritual point of view?

Bad fruit is sometimes easy to spot. It looks bad, smells bad, taste bad and is rotten to the core. However, because we are continually in a spiritual battle, our adversary will camouflage bad fruit so that it looks enticing. Remember Jesus warned us that we are to serve God and not money. See Matthew 6:24. Jesus tells us that we are not to be concerned with material possessions or even to be concerned with what we eat drink or ware. I think that by becoming concerned with material possessions and listening to those who espouse the prosperity gospel, we are giving in to and seeking false prophets. After all, false prophets come in sheep's clothing seeking to deceive and to obstruct what is true.

I have watched television preachers who give a very subtle message of prosperity. By doing that they are bringing in many people and are amassing large fortunes. Jesus said to beware of these false prophets because they dress in sheep's clothing, and their message is as subtle as Satan's message to Eve in the garden.

It is so easy to become overwhelmed with advertising on television and on other social media. We are being told that if we want to be happy and get along with others, we need to buy this or that product. Billions of dollars are spent trying to convince us to buy something because everybody else is buying and using that product. I am not saying that we should not dress nicely, eat good food and exercise in order to keep ourselves healthy. However, when we become obsessed with our appearances and even our health, we run the risk of being overwhelmed with things rather than with the spiritual side of our life.

How do we keep in touch with our spiritual selves? How do we keep ourselves in close communication with God? Are we in fact storing up treasures for ourselves in heaven? Can we detect a false prophet from those who are speaking spiritual truths? Have our lives become so filled with our possessions, money, emotions, and all sorts of distractions that we neglect the good gifts that our heavenly Father wants to bestow on us?

Maybe it was easier for previous generations to understand their spiritual selves. Maybe modern society has become so complex that our spirituality has become lost or at least hard to find. Does our current state of affairs remind you of Jesus's words in the parable of the sower of seeds? Remember that some of the seeds fell among the thorns and thistles? Jesus told his disciples that the cares of the world would choke out the development of the gospel message. We should all take into consideration these words and be careful that our spiritual lives are not overcome by the pursuit of earthly treasures.

Chapter 15
Do We All Have a Spiritual Life?

Throughout this book, I have discussed the place of the Holy Spirit in a Christian's life. As I was thinking about the place of the Holy Spirit in the lives of Christians, it occurred to me to ask, does everyone, Christians and non- Christians, have a spiritual life?

When we were children or even in our adult years, before Christ took up residence in our lives, we would get in trouble, and we would know that we had done something wrong. I believe that we have a conscience at an early stage of our development. The conscience is an internal mechanism that lets us know right from wrong. The conscience is not the spiritual part of our life. The conscience is a part of our socialization, which allows us to adapt to societal norms. Earlier we discussed Sigmund Freud's theory that everyone had an id, an ego, and a superego. In Freud's thought the conscience was found in an individual's superego. The superego caused a person to subdue his/her self-gratification instincts that in all likelihood, brought that individual into conflict with others.

Without a conscience, there would be complete anarchy, and everybody would be willing to kill his brother because he had offered a better sacrifice. The conscience functions somewhat similarly to that aspect of the Holy Spirit that warns us of temptations that we need to be careful of and hopefully overcome, but it is not the Holy Spirit, and it is not the spiritual side of our life to which I am referring in this chapter. Remember the Holy Spirit is a seal of the presence of Jesus in a Christian's life and is not found in non-Christians. It is my contention that all people have a spiritual part of their personality but only Christians have the Holy Spirit dwelling in them.

Many years ago, I became involved with a wrongful death action in which my client's son was killed. The young man was a passenger in the car being driven by his brother. They were on their way to the Atlanta airport to pick up their mother who was flying in from Chicago. The young man was killed when his brother drove into the back of a truck that had broken down and was parked on Interstate 75 during a heavy rainstorm.

I had known Bob for a couple of years, and the death of his son, in that tragic accident, took an extreme emotional toll on the whole family. I learned that Bob had moved to St. Petersburg, Florida, and it became necessary for me to travel to Tampa / Saint Pete to help prepare Bob for the upcoming trial. Bob and his new wife allowed me to stay in their apartment and invited me to attend their church while I was there.

Bob and his wife attended the Spiritualist church. I had never been to that particular denomination and was very unfamiliar with their beliefs and how their church service was conducted. Bob had become one of the leaders of the church. During the church service that I attended, Bob was called upon to assist other church members in finding their spiritual guides. Quickly I realized I was not in a Christian church and that their beliefs were at odds with my beliefs.

Bob told me that he could read people's auras. He told me that everybody emitted an aura that appeared to him in distinct colors. Bob said that he could read these auras and that he could assist people to find their spiritual guides to lead them on their life's journey. Much of Bob's beliefs were so foreign to me that I had a hard time staying in the service. Eventually, I got up and went outside to wait for Bob and his wife to take me back to their apartment. You could say that Bob had a heightened since of spirituality.

Later, Bob and his wife moved back to Atlanta and invited me and my ex-wife Ileana, to dinner at their apartment. My wife, Ileana, very much believed in astrology and other supernatural phenomenon and was very impressed with Bob and his wife. My marriage to Ileana ended as a result of her beliefs in astrology and the kind of spirituality that Bob preached. I do not know if that form of spirituality was fake or had some basis in the occult. I do know that the spirituality that formed the basis of Bob's religion was not of God. Whether Bob's religion was Satanic, I leave to my readers decision. I do know that I could not be around that form of spirituality to which I was subjected that evening in St. Petersburg, Florida.

Jesus said that God is spirit. In John 4:7-26 Jesus encounters a Samaritan woman after His disciples had gone into the nearby town of Sychar to buy food. The woman had come to the town's well in order to draw water to take back to her home. Jesus asked this woman to give Him a drink. The woman was shocked that a Jewish man would be asking a Samaritan woman to give Him a drink of water because generally the Jews had nothing to do with the Samaritans. In that story, Jesus tells the woman that if she knew who she was talking to, she would be asking Jesus to provide to her with living water, a water that had a quality that would bring about eternal life. The woman was not fully satisfied with Jesus's explanation of living water. Finally, Jesus tells her that a time is coming when, "True worshipers will worship the Father in the Spirit and in truth, for they are the kind of worshippers the Father seeks. God is spirit, and His worshippers must worship in the Spirit and in truth."

The Bible tells us that God has created mankind in His own image. Genesis 1:27 says, "So God created mankind in His own image, in the image of God created He them; Male and female He created them." If God is spirit, then He must have created me with a spirit that is able to connect with God. When I worship God, I worship Him in spirit and in truth. When I pray, my spirit reaches out to God to seek a connection with Him. When God answers my prayers, I am called upon to see God's spirit moving in my life. These are certainly spiritual matters that requires that I have a spiritual understanding, hear with spiritual ears, and seeing with spiritual eyes. We will talk about spiritual wisdom, spiritual hearing, and spiritual seeing a little later.

In Psalms 51, David, after he has recognized his sin because of his affair with Bathsheba, asks God to, "Create in me a clean heart Oh God and renew a right spirit within me." David had the expectation that God would set his spirit right even in light of David's adultery and murder. Should we not also expect God to answer our prayers when we pray with the right spirit and ask God to renew a right spirit in us?

So, the easy answer to my first question, "Do all people have a spirit?," is yes, we all have a spirit. The next question is, does my spirit have a godly nature? As we have learned, some people are godly, and some people not so much. Remember, earlier in this book we looked at the heroes of faith listed in Hebrews 11. One of the characteristics of those who had great faith is that they are godly people. A godly person not only has great faith, but is willing to step out on that faith, keep God's commandments, live a righteous life, have a pure heart, and is willing to suffer for his faith.

How do I receive a godly spirit? Jesus tells His disciples at John 16 that He will send to them the Holy Spirit. The Holy Spirit will be able to teach His disciples because He is the spirit of truth and a spirit that will glorify Jesus. At John 17, Jesus prays for His disciples very shortly before his death and resurrection. In that prayer, which I encourage you to read along with reading what I am writing, Jesus prays that His disciples will be protected from the evil one, that they will be able to endure the hatred that they will surely encounter, and that they will be sent into the world as God has sent Jesus into the world. Then at John 17:20 Jesus expands those He is praying for to include Christians that will come afterward, including me. "My prayer is not for them alone. I pray also for those who will believe in me through their (the disciples) message, that all of them may be one, Father, just as you are in me, and I am in you. May they also be in us so that the world may believe that you have sent me. I have given them the glory that you gave me that they may be one as we are one- I in them and you in me- so that they may be brought to complete unity. Then the world will know that you sent me and have loved them even as you have loved me."

Jesus tells the world that those who believe in Him, Christians, can rely on the fact that Jesus is in them and that they are in Jesus. Later, Paul expresses this truth at 2 Corinthians 5:17 when he says, "Therefore, if anyone is in Christ, the new creation has come: the old has gone, the new is here! All this is from God, who reconciled Himself to us through Christ and gave us the ministry of reconciliation: that God was reconciling the world to Himself in Christ not counting people's sins against them." What this means is that when I accept Christ and believe that He is the Son of God, the Holy Spirit comes into me, and my spirit is able to communicate with and reconcile me to God. We would express that in today's language as, "I am synchronized by the Holy Spirit and with God. Me and God have synced up."

If God has made me in His image, and that image includes His spirit, then God is willing to share His separate and distinct Holy Spirit with me when I accept and ask Jesus to come into my life. My spirit then is in synchronization with God, and I can live a godly life. Without the presence of Jesus, my spiritual self still exists but it does not have the quality of godliness that is necessary for me to be a person of great faith, and I have not received eternal life. What is really the most important consequence of my relationship with Jesus Christ, is that I have an assurance from the moment of my acceptance of Him that Jesus is in me and that I am in Him and that we are in God.

Chapter 16
I Have Joy Down in My Heart

Jesus told His disciples in John 16:18-28 that He would be soon leaving them and going to the Father. Because of this teaching the disciples were disheartened. The disciples were told that the world would rejoice at their grief. Then Jesus says, but soon I am going to return to you so that you will have joy. Jesus then tells His disciples that up until this time they have been asking Jesus questions but that they would no longer have to do that because Jesus would be with the Father and that the Father loved them, and they would share in God's love because Jesus was sending His Holy Spirit to fill the disciples with joy.

Early in the book of Mark, Jesus goes to the river Jordan to be baptized by John the Baptist. John tells Jesus that Jesus does not need to be baptized by John to which Jesus replies, (Matthew 3: 15) "Let it be so now; It is proper for us to do this to fulfill all righteousness." Mark says and as Jesus was coming out of the water, heaven was torn open, and the Spirit could be seen descending on Jesus like a dove. Then a voice came from heaven saying, "You are my Son, whom I love; With you I am well pleased." The relationship between Jesus and the heavenly Father was and is intimate. There is a love bond between Jesus and God.

Later, in Luke 9:28-36 (see also Mark 9:2-8; and Matthew 17:1-8) Jesus takes Peter, John, and James with Him up a mountain to pray. While they were praying, suddenly Jesus's appearance changed. His face became radiant, and His clothes became as bright as a flash of lightning. Then Moses and Elijah appeared also in glorious splendor talking with Jesus. A cloud then covered the mountain and a voice from heaven declared, "This is my son, whom I have chosen; listen to him."

The intimacy between Jesus and God was probably not as clear to His disciples as it should have been at His baptism and when He was transfigured on the mountain. We have the perspective of history, and the ability to read what happened at Jesus's baptism and at the transfiguration. By the time that Jesus was preparing for His crucifixion, His disciples had been with Him for some time, and they were able to understand the intimacy between Jesus and God to some extent but not fully. Jesus still had to tell His disciples that the relationship between Jesus and God was such that God had sent Jesus into the world, and that Jesus was preparing to go back to God. Jesus then tells His disciples that while they would grieve for a little while that their joy would become great because Jesus was coming back. Jesus would physically come back for a period of time, but more importantly Jesus was going to send to the disciples, a Comforter, an Advocate, the Spirit of Truth, His Holy Spirit.

The Holy Spirit is a part of the Holy Trinity, Father, Son and Holy Spirit. When we accept Jesus into our lives, we are sealed by the Holy Spirit. (Ephesians 1:13) That means, Jesus is in me, and I am in Jesus and because Jesus and the Father are one, then I have a close loving relationship with God as well. John expresses this in his gospel at John 3:16, "For God so loved the world that He gave His only begotten son, that whosoever believes in Him shall not perish but have everlasting life." Further, in 1 John 1:1-4 the apostle and perhaps closest friend of Jesus while He was on earth, says, "That which was from the beginning, which we have heard, which we have seen with our own eyes, which we have looked at and our hands have touched- this we proclaim concerning the Word of life . The life appeared; we have seen it and testified to it, and we proclaim to you the eternal life, which was with the Father and has appeared to us. We proclaim to you what we have seen and heard, so that you also may have fellowship with us. And our fellowship is with the Father and with the Son, Jesus Christ. We write this to make our joy complete."

The apostle John probably wrote the gospel of John and 1 John many years after Jesus's death and resurrection. John had years to think about the time that he spent with Jesus. John's encounter with Jesus was more than a Damascus Road experience, but in a sense, it was also like the encounter Paul had with Jesus. John says that he saw Him in person, and his hands reached out and touched Jesus in His bodily form. John thinking back to those days when Jesus was still on earth thinks about the words that Jesus spoke and the meaning of those words. It is as if John had a revelation about all that had happened from the time that Jesus called him while he was fishing in Galilee until the time of the crucifixion.

John undoubtedly had time to remember the time that he and Peter raced each other to the tomb to which Jesus was taken after His crucifixion. John was there with Jesus as He preached to the multitudes, healed thousands, cast out many demons, was with Jesus when Jesus was transfigured, and was obviously there when Jesus ascended back to the Father just as Jesus had said He would.

John speaks to us about the testimony that has come to him through the water, the blood and the Spirit. The testimony of each of these points to the relationship between God and man. The baptism of Jesus was for the proclamation that God's spirit would descend like a dove on the Son that God had sent into the world. The crucifixion of Jesus required the shedding of blood for the redemption of our sins. The water and the blood signify the extent to which God expressed the humanity of Jesus as God's presence in the world. The Spirit as it descended on Jesus at His baptism testifies that God's love is in the very person of Jesus for the world to see and accept.

John then tells us that, "Whoever believes in the Son of God accepts this testimony. Whoever does not believe God has made Him out to be a liar, because they have not believed the testimony God has given about His Son. And this is the testimony: God has given us eternal life, and this life is in His Son. Whoever has the Son has life; whoever does not have the Son of God does not have life." 1 John 5:10-12.

Our joy is in the fact that Jesus as a human being was baptized and shed His blood in the presence of mankind. Our joy is completed by the fact that the divinity of Jesus has also shown through to mankind by His resurrection and return to the heavenly Father. Our joy is extended by the promise of eternal life by our acceptance of Jesus into our lives. When Jesus came into my life, I became a new creation. The old self continues to fade away. The relationship with God becomes more and more intimate. The love that God has for His Son is directed to that part of me that is the dwelling place of the Holy Spirit.

Yes, each of us has a spirit. That spirit yearns for a connection with God. We are incomplete without the presence of the Holy Spirit in our lives. I pray that you receive the joy of your salvation by surrendering your life to Jesus and asking for the presence of the Holy Spirit.

Chapter 17
The Wisdom That Comes From God

When I was a child and would say something smart back to my father he would say, "What, are you a wise guy?" He meant that in a derogatory manner. Today we would call a person that my father called a wise guy, a "smart ass." You may have guessed by now that there were periods of time in my life in which I was referred to as a "smart ass." There have been a few times (very few indeed) in which people thought I was just plain smart. There were a few times when I was astonished by what people thought of me.

In the late 1980s, I had a big case in federal court against the Ford Motor Company. Ford had hired well respected lawyers in Atlanta to defend the case that I brought. The case involved serious injuries to young sailors who were traveling from their basic training in Cherry Point, North Carolina to their first duty station in Jacksonville, Florida. As they traveled down I-95, they had a blowout on their right rear tire. The car that they were driving, a 1982 Ford Escort, began to fishtail and eventually flipped and rolled over many times on the I-95 pavement. The driver of the car was Gary Hardison, and as a result of the rolling over of the car he was ejected and landed in the middle of I-95. Gary suffered a traumatic brain injury that left him seriously impaired. One of the most catastrophic events that can occur in a car wreck is for the car to roll-over because that event will more than likely cause brain injury.

We hired experts to reconstruct the events that caused the car to roll-over. It was determined that there was a failure of the right rear strut to which the right rear tire was attached. We also determined that the geometry of the Ford Escort automobile was such that when the car went into a slide that geometry caused a jacking effect, similar to the force of a pole vault, which flipped the car and caused it to roll- over. One of the telling pieces of evidence that the experts used to determine why the car flipped and rolled was the broken strut that had been taken from the wreckage.

During the trial of the case, I placed the broken strut into evidence so that it could be taken by the jury into the jury room during their consideration of the case. During the defendant's part of the case, Ford decided to put into evidence a brand-new strut. I made a strenuous objection to Ford's attempt to put the new strut into evidence. We argued both sides of that issue to the judge for over an hour. Eventually, the judge allowed Ford to put the new strut into evidence. I believed that it was error for the judge to admit the new strut into evidence and felt that my case was somewhat damaged by that event.

The case finally went to the jury for determination of whether Ford was liable for the injuries to Gary Hardison or not. After about three hours of deliberation the jury returned a verdict in favor of Gary for a substantial amount of money. I was elated. My clients were very happy.

As I was packing up my papers and evidence after the trial, I was called out into the hallway because the foreman of the jury wanted to speak to me. The jury foreman told me that I was a very smart man (the actual term he used was "sly dog" which are the words used in Atlanta for smart person) because I had allowed the introduction of the brand-new strut.

The jury foreman told me that it was because the jury was able to compare the difference between the strut taken off the wreck and that brand-new strut that the jury was able to return a verdict in my client's favor. I did not have the heart to tell the jury foreman that I was such a "sly dog" that I had argued against the introduction of the brand-new strut. I thought to myself, "yeah you are a real sly dog, you really know how to persuade a jury."

I say all that in order to assure you that when we think we are very smart or have sufficient wisdom, the exact opposite may be true. There have been other times when I thought that I had done a really dumb thing only to find out that it turned out OK. The question that I asked myself, are there very different kinds of wisdom and if so, what is the difference?

Some say that the smartest man to ever live was King Solomon. Solomon was the son of David and Bathsheba. His older brother tried to overthrow King David but was killed during the uprising. David, perhaps the greatest of the Jewish kings decided that Solomon would be his successor. The Bible records at 1 Kings 3:1 through 15 that after Solomon became king, he did what was right in the sight of God and traveled to Gibeon to offer sacrifices. Evidently, God was pleased with Solomon and told Solomon that whatever you ask for I will give you. Solomon replied acknowledging that God had shown great kindness to David and now to Solomon. Solomon acknowledged that he was lacking in discernment to distinguish between what was right and what was wrong in the governance of the people of Israel, and asked God for wisdom in order to justly lead the people. God was pleased with the choice that Solomon had made. A gift of discernment from

God can therefore be thought of as one of the attributes of wisdom.

Fundamentally, discernment is the ability to determine whether the people that we are dealing with are doing what is right or are doing what is wrong. At Hosea 14:9 the scripture says, "Who is wise? Let them realize these things. Who is discerning? Let them understand. The ways of the Lord are right; The righteous walk in them but the rebellious stumbled in them." While these words seem clear enough, you know I am going to have a question. That is; what are the ways of the Lord that Hosea is talking about? Therefore, I had to re-read Hosea and found that the ways of the Lord contained in that prophecy concern how people treat the poor and whether people are being fair those in need. From that I surmised that a part of wisdom is how we treat others and whether we are being fair in all our dealings especially with the poor.

At John 2:24-25 the Bible tells us that when Jesus was in His early ministry and was in Jerusalem for the festival of the Passover; He did many signs and people began to believe in Jesus. But Jesus did not entrust Himself to the people because He knew all people and could see what was in their hearts. Jesus had great spiritual discernment and wisdom concerning what was going on in people's minds and hearts. When we get to the Book of Revelation, Jesus tells the church at Thyatira that He, whose eyes are like burning fire, can see through the hearts and minds of all people and is thus able to discern who they really are. Being able to understand where people are really coming from and what their intent is, is the value of having discernment (wisdom) that comes from God.

Paul at 1 Thessalonians 5:21 tells those who belonged to that church should not quench the Spirit. But the church should test all prophecies to determine whether they are good and they should reject that which is evil. That scripture indicates that there is a spiritual wisdom that Paul is calling on the church to invoke in order to embrace what is good and to eschew what is evil.

From this it is clear to me, and I hope to you also, that there is a wisdom that comes from God that is not like earthly wisdom. I was watching a television program in which a person who was nicknamed "the Beast" was heavily engaged in trivia. The show's contestants were pitted against "the Beast" in order to gain prizes. Whoever answered the most questions, had the most knowledge of the subject matter, within the time allowed by the game won the prize. We often equate knowledge with wisdom. Knowledge and wisdom are not of equal value. It is true that we must have knowledge of what is going on around us including how to make a living in order to survive. Wisdom is much different from knowledge.

The wisdom that comes from God allows us to discern whether the people that we are dealing with are godly or are faking it. (My son tells me that the word for fakers is posers). This ability to discern is an integral part of the wisdom that God wishes to provide to us. In James 1:5, the scripture says, "If any of you lacks wisdom, you should ask God, who gives generously to all without finding fault, and it will be given to you. But when you ask, you must believe and not doubt, because the one who doubts is like a wave of the sea, blown and tossed in the wind. That person should not expect to receive anything from the Lord. Such a person is double minded and unstable in all they do."

James, who is also called "old camel knees," because he stayed on his knees in prayer for long periods of time, was also a close associate of Jesus, when Jesus was in his earthly ministry. James was one of the three disciples that accompanied Jesus to the mount of transfiguration that we discussed earlier. This James was one of the leaders of the church in Jerusalem. If James says God generously provides wisdom to those who ask, I think that he was talking from his own experience. James says that if we ask God for wisdom that God provides wisdom to us without looking as to whether we are faulty individuals (which we all are). I take that to mean that even in our sinful nature God is willing to grant us wisdom, because having people who want to do right is within God's purpose for our lives. Think of how that happens. If we were asking God for wisdom, we must believe that there is a God. If we are asking of God, we must have confidence that He hears our prayers and that He will respond. In this case James says that God will respond generously to those asking for wisdom. What is inferred by this is that the person asking for wisdom is a person with faith and is therefore godly.

The caveat to seeking wisdom from God, is that the person asking for wisdom must have an expectation that God will provide the wisdom that you are seeking. It is evident to me, that the wisdom that God provides is spiritual wisdom and that wisdom is very different from what the world associates with those who may possess a very high IQ.

Jesus on many occasions told His disciples that they needed to hear what He was telling them. As you may recall after telling the parable of the sower, Jesus told His disciples that He was speaking in parables because what He was saying would be hidden from many that were listening to Him. He specifically told His disciples that they should hear what He was saying with an understanding that Jesus was going to give them. In Revelations 2 and 3, Jesus has specific messages to the churches to which He was writing. At the end of each of those messages, Jesus tells the congregations that, "Let anyone who has ears to hear listen to what the spirit says to the churches."

One of the methods by which we gain an understanding is by hearing the words of Jesus. In order to hear the words of Jesus we must listen with spiritual ears so that we will obtain a spiritual wisdom. If you truly want to know what God expects of you, you must have an understanding, a wisdom, that only God can provide. Gladly, God will generously give us wisdom if we ask for it with an expectation that our prayers will be answered and that we will receive godly wisdom.

What can you do with that wisdom that God provides? He who has ears let him hear what the spirit is saying. Jesus tells His disciples that they must listen with spiritual ears. If I am a disciple of Jesus, I must also listen with spiritual ears. Listening to what the spirit is saying requires prayerful, focused attention. Jesus said that, if anyone wished to follow Jesus, they must take up their cross and follow.

Chapter 18
Following Jesus

A few years ago, there was a movement in the United States In which people would wear arm bracelets with the letters WWJD inscribed. Those letters stood for the words, "what would Jesus do." I recall that even the preacher at my church wore such a wristband. I think it is significant that people were asking, "what would Jesus do?" I have often wondered where individuals discerned what actions Jesus would have taken in any particular circumstance. Later I read a book by Phillip Yancey titled, The Jesus I Never Knew. In that book, Yancey gives a perspective of how the life of Jesus, His teachings, the miracles He performed, and His death and resurrection have impacted the author and even civilization as we know it.

Jesus of Nazareth, the historical figure, has had a significant impact on western civilization. When I was a freshman in college, one of the required readings in a class, that was entitled "Western Civilization," was a book by Roland Bainton. The book was The Horizon History of Christianity. That book traced the impact of Christianity in Europe and especially in The United States. When I was in law school in New Orleans, I attended St. Charles Avenue Baptist Church. The pastor, Avery Lee, was a graduate of the Yale divinity school. One of his professors was Roland Bainton. One Sunday morning Pastor Lee invited Professor Bainton to preach. Because I had previously read his book, I was enthralled to have the chance to meet Professor Bainton.

At times when I prepare to teach my Sunday school lessons, I think of the impact that Christianity has had on my life. I have been able to read the Bible in the English language. That ability was not given to many Christians until late in the Middle Ages. The Catholic Church at one time prohibited the printing of the Bible in vernacular language. Spanish law in the 1400's prohibited the Bible from being printed in Spanish even at the time that Columbus sailed the ocean blue. There were Baptist martyrs who smuggled the Bible into England so that common people would be able to read the Bible for themselves.

I am free not only to read the Bible, but I am also free to interpret the Bible as the Holy Spirit gives me understanding. That has not always been the case. Even today there are those who are dogmatic in their interpretation of the Bible and who would insist that others adhere to their orthodoxy. Fortunately, I live in the United States and the Constitution's Bill of Rights prohibits any government from taking away my right to read and interpret the Bible for myself.

These freedoms and many more are a result of the impact of Christianity.

Equally as important, Christianity has had an economic impact on western civilization. History tells us that the Protestant Reformation produced capitalism. The "Protestant work ethic," as historical economist explains, became the driving force for the American economy for a long period of America's history. Christianity, in my opinion, set the regulated economy in motion. While I believe that is a very important topic to discuss, I will have to wait for another day to discuss those topics. Suffice it to say that the impact of Christianity on western civilization has been the most important driving force for our modern culture. What the impact of Christianity will continue to have, is a matter of speculation. My speculation, however, is that the Kingdom of God will continue to produce the effects that God intends because ultimately God is in control of the future.

So, what am I to do? Jesus said at Luke 9:23, "Whoever wants to be my disciple must deny themselves and take up their cross daily and follow me. For whoever wants to save their life will lose it, but whoever loses their life for me will save it. What good is it for someone to gain the whole world, and yet lose or forfeit their very self? Whoever is ashamed of me and of my words, the Son of Man will be ashamed of them when He comes in His glory and in the glory of the Father and of the holy angels."

Paul says it this way, "Therefore, I urge you brothers and sisters, in view of God's mercy, to offer your bodies as a living sacrifice, holy and pleasing to God- this is your true and proper worship. Do not conform to the pattern of this world but be transformed by the renewing of your mind. Then you will be able to test and approve what God's will is- His good, pleasing and perfect will." Romans 12:1-2

The instructions that Jesus (and Paul) require, taking up a cross and offering myself as a sacrifice. Does that sound like a lot of trouble to you? The cross that Jesus is referring to is the instrument of torture and death that the Roman Empire used in order to force Rome's will on the population. A living sacrifice that Paul alludes to, especially in the Old Testament, required that a living child be thrown into a fire. How can we possibly come to an understanding of the meaning of these commands?

It is important to note that in both instances, Jesus and Paul are saying that the person that wants to be a disciple of Jesus must voluntarily take extreme measures in order to comply with the direction that Jesus is clearly giving. Jesus did not say I am going to put you on a cross. Jesus does say that if you want to be a disciple you must voluntarily submit to the same life that Jesus lived while He was among us. The characteristics of that life was that Jesus healed the sick, comforted those who were in need, called on people to repent, preached that the Kingdom of God was at hand, gave His life up for our sins, and rose from the dead in order to return to God.

After meeting Jesus on the road to Damascus Paul did the very same acts that Jesus did. Paul went about preaching the gospel and telling people to repent and to accept Jesus as their savior. Paul sacrificed himself for the cause of Jesus. I once had the opportunity to travel to Spain. I flew to Madrid and rented a car and drove toward Lisbon, Portugal. I eventually came to Media, a town in the Extremadura region of Spain. While I was exploring that town, I came on the ruins of ancient Roman buildings. One of those buildings was an old Roman temple to one of their Pagan gods. I then came to the Roman amphitheater and noticed that there was a plaque on the wall of the stage that said that Paul had preached there. I was excited to have stood were Paul stood.

I remembered that Paul had been arrested in Jerusalem by the Romans because he had started a riot among the Jews. I think the Jews recognized that Paul was the same Paul that once had the responsibility of persecuting Christ's followers. Now those very same Jews understood that Paul was a very differed man. The change in Paul was complete. Paul the persecutor had become the servant of Jesus. The very same Jesus that those in authority despised, hated, and put to death on a Roman cross. Paul because he was willing to risk everything he had for the cause of Christ, had incurred the hatred of the same people that had mattered most to him before Paul met Jesus on the road to Damascus. Paul had been ambitious and expected that he would go far in the Jewish community until he met Jesus. Paul gave his own ambitions up in order to follow Jesus because of Jesus's personal appeal to Paul. Paul was willing to give up his own ambitions and to submit to the authority of Christ. That made all the difference and actually set the course of western civilization.

What does it mean to take up your cross? It means to follow Jesus by giving yourself fully and without reservation to the direction of the Holy Spirit. How do you know the direction of the Holy Spirit? Some people say, "you know it when you see it." That brings to my mind the idea that we all have a history in our relationships with the Holy Spirit. I often tell my Sunday school class, that if you think about what has gone on in your life you can look back and see the hand of the Holy Spirit directing your actions. I know that is true in my life and I believe it is probably true in the lives of everyone that has committed themselves to Jesus.

I think of the time when I was in law school and was looking for a summer job. I prayed. Out of the blue I got a call from the director of the Baptist Student Union who wanted to know if I would be interested in taking a position as a Summer Missionary in Washington DC. The job required me to work in the office of Senator Edmund Muskie, and also to work on weekends at the Johenning Community Center in Anacostia. Needless to say, I felt as if my prayer had been answered. Not only was I getting a job for the summer, but it was also going to be a very exciting and fulfilling time in my life.

I worked as a legislative aide on Capitol Hill. I helped write speeches for the senator. I helped organize a meeting between Senator Muskie and some of the leading economist in the United States. On weekends I would drive the community center's van to Lorton prison to pick up men who were being furloughed for the purpose of helping children to learn to read. On Sunday the group of summer missionaries to which I belonged, would help in local churches, and eventually I would drive the prisoners back to Lorton.

The children at the Community Center in Anacostia had not been around white people. The little children were amazed at the amount of hair I had on my arms and legs. They would often come up to me and rub me and ask, "how did you get so furry?" That summer was one of the happiest of my life and I am convinced that it was the work of the Holy Spirit that placed me in Washington DC and at the Community Center in Anacostia.

I am sure that if you think back in your Christian pilgrimage, you will be able to remember times when you are absolutely sure that you too were under the leadership of the Holy Spirit. We all have a history with the Holy Spirit's work in our lives. If not, you need to ask Jesus into your life now!!!

There have been other times when I have felt the leadership of the Holy Spirit. I pray on a regular basis that I will be able to step aside from my own interests and submit myself to the leadership that Jesus demands of me. Taking up His cross, requires a committed effort to subdue my desire to be in control and instead put myself under His control. While that may sound easy, it is a constant struggle to tell myself to get out of the way and let the leadership of the Holy Spirit take charge. I believe even Paul, who saw the great light and clearly heard the words of Jesus, at times struggled with giving up his own self interests. It is part of human nature to want to be in control, not only of ourselves, but also of those over whom we have influence. In those situations, we must also remember that I am not the only one that Jesus is interested in leading. Jesus has a plan for all His followers. Sometimes it is necessary for me to wait on the Holy Spirit to act in my life.

When do we know that we are under the leadership of the Holy Spirit? If we are willing to give up our own selves and submit ourselves to Jesus, we will be led by the Holy Spirit. Of that, I am sure.

Jesus Christ loved us so much that He came down from heaven in order to show us His love. He willfully went to the cross, He suffered and died for my sins, and He arose again. He is alive now and calls each of us to love Him and to show that love to others. Jesus has given us the Holy Spirit so that we can be in Him and He in us and we can experience Jesus's is love now and forever. Nothing can separate us from love of Jesus.

Paul says it best at Romans 8:31. "What, then, shall we say in response to these things? If God is for us, who can be against us? He did not spare His own son, but gave Him up for us all- how will He not also, along with Him, graciously give us all things? Who can bring any charge against those whom God has chosen? It is God who justifies. Who then is the one who condemns? No one. Christ Jesus who died- more than that, who was raised to life- is at the right hand of God and is also interceding for us. Who shall separate us from the love of Christ? Shall trouble or hardship or persecution or famine or nakedness or danger or sword? As it is written: 'For your sake we face death all day long; we are considered as sheep to be slaughtered.' No, in all these things we are more than conquerors through Him who loved us. For I am convinced that neither death nor life, neither angels nor demons, neither the present nor the future, nor any powers, neither height nor depth, nor anything else in all creation, will be able to separate us from the love of God that is in Christ Jesus our Lord." Amen, and again I say Amen.

Acknowledgement

I want to express my grateful thanks too several individuals who have helped me in the writing and preparation of this book. First of all, I wish to gratefully thank my daughter, Alison Sakas Hardwick and her family Who allowed me to stay in Burnsville, Mississippi while I was researching and writing this book. Without her and her family's gracious accommodation the writing of this book would not have been possible. Additionally, I also am grateful to Pastor Jon Haimes In the congregation of the Glendale Baptist Church in Glen, Mississippi for allowing me to use their facilities and Internet connections while I worked on this book. I'm especially thankful to pastor John Haimes who also read an early draft of this book and encouraged me to continue.

I have dedicated this book to my best friend Patavia, who has been more than encouraging in the writing and research that I have used in order to complete this work. She has been inspirational to me on many occasions when I thought I would just give up and do something else.

I would also like to thank the members of the Sunday school class that I taught while attending Glendale Baptist. They were a great encouragement to me Throughout the time that I was conducting Sunday school at their church. I used the Sunday school class as a sounding board for some of the ideas that I have expressed in various chapters throughout this book. Without their attention and willingness to hear what I had to say and on occasion a few corny jokes as well, the writing of this book would not have been nearly as much fun as it turned out to be.

I am eternally grateful to the Lord Jesus Christ and the presence of the Holy Spirit in my life. On many occasions while I was engaged in the writing I was encouraged and enlightened by His presents and instruction. It always seemed that when I had reached a stumbling block that the Holy Spirit would speak to me and give me an idea as to where to go as I continued to write. Without the presence of the Holy Spirit leading me this book could not have been completed. I thank God daily for Jesus Christ and His presence in my life.

Printed by Libri Plureos GmbH in Hamburg, Germany